D1117210

Strategies for Teaching Christian Adults

268.08
W64s

11.01

Strategies for Teaching Christian Adults

Warren W. Wilbert

Baker Book House
Grand Rapids, Michigan 49506

75961

Copyright 1984 by
Baker Book House Company
ISBN: 0-8010-9668-5
Printed in the United States of America

To
Doctors **Fred Kramer** and **Henry J. Eggold:**
Friends,
Colleagues,
Brothers in the Faith

Contents

22   2710

List of Figures

An Open Letter of Introduction

Dear Reader:

For some time now I have contended that what passes for teaching and learning in adult Bible classes is a pale reflection of teaching and learning at its best. I wonder if you wouldn't agree that there really is a gap between potential and productivity wide enough to make us all wonder about the good intentions, continual pleading, hours of preparation, and expensive resources lavished on those Sunday morning or weekday evening sessions. Surely all that effort and time ought to produce more than a ho-hum here and there!

Although I realize there are a number of variables worth considering, I've singled out one of them and have tried to contribute something I hope is both important and helpful in equipping the saints. So we're going to take a look at the variable of ways and means to go about Bible class work, keeping not only the teacher in mind, but also those who sit in class, Bibles and notebooks at the ready.

What I am going to share is based on a conviction that both teachers and learners are made, not born. And if that conviction rests on a solid foundation in educational principle, as I'm sure it does, then surely a searching look at what each is doing is in order. What we do, that is, *the way* we approach and work through Bible studies is a concern often overlooked and lost in the shuffle of content, facts, and conclusions. I do not mean to minimize their importance, but I do mean to call attention to these other concerns you yourself cannot help but have experienced as either beneficial or detrimental to the whole Bible class scenario.

I would also dare to hope that what lies ahead is relatively jargon-free. Toward that end I have even used terms interchangeably in an attempt to reduce the friction that often arises when the more casual among us are suddenly confronted with a variety of terms that look suspiciously alike, yet turn out, later on, to be miles apart. A case in point: the terms "method" and "strategy," which get the full treatment of definition and differentiation in more formalized academic settings, appear as "merely" synonymous. I am running the risk of muddying scholarly waters simply because the message, from my point of view, is so important that it shouldn't get lost or belabored in a mountain of detail and technicalities. Perhaps that may offend you a bit. If it does, by all means take pen in hand and contribute your own talents to this vital and indispensable foundation piece of Christian education.

Finally, a word or two about the three major strategies awaiting your examination. You will not fail to notice that each contains a number of additional approaches to Bible class activity *within* its structure, which gives me an opportunity to incorporate still more variety into the plan of action. Lecture/discussion, skill mastery, and case studies form the three basic approaches to study considered, but in each instance there is sufficient allowance for additions or variations within the sequences provided. One special note: in many of the case studies presented, the Scripture readings lead Bible class members up to the point of a problem or issue but do not include the verses that actually, in many instances, contain solutions. In social work for educational purposes, that is what is known as an open case study. I'm sure you will deal with that in your own way.

I wish you good reading ahead. My prayer is that you and yours, and all those dedicated, deserving folks in your Bible classes, will be blessed mightily as you constantly seek to build Christ's kingdom and nurture His people!

Sincerely,

Warren N. Wilbert

Part

Adult Bible Class
Strategies Reconsidered

Following a particularly galling defeat the coach stormed out on to the practice field, gathered the team around him, picked up the nearest ball, and thundered: "This is a ball!" The squad knew exactly what that meant: back to square one, fundamentals and basic plays; in sum, starting over and getting it right!

In some respects those of us involved in adult Christian education need a review of fundamentals, just like that team gathered around the coach. For us, too, it does not seem out of place to suggest that review, rethinking, and reevaluation are in order. If our aim is to become more effectively productive in the majestic responsibility of building Christ's Body, it won't hurt a bit to take another searching look; it can only help. But where to look? The suggestions in this initial section focus on some fundamental variables at work in the Bible class, that familiar wheelhorse of adult Christian education. One in particular may seem embarrassingly fundamental: method.

Who needs a review or rethinking of method, you say? The first few items under investigation contend for just such review, especially inasmuch as they seldom surface in the thinking of Bible class administrators and practitioners. They are considerations such as How do Christian adults learn most effectively? Which are the prime and influential concerns governing the choice of method? What are the characteristics of the two basic styles in methodology, presentation, and exploration? The key to personal involvement and application, a commitment to purposeful and skilled activity, and a vital, dedicated interest in becoming a knowledgeable worker in Christ's kingdom—all this and surely more—is wrapped up in the *how* of nurturing process.

Along with other contributing factors, method is an invaluable, strategic part of nurture in the church. It is this aspect of the process, then, that we intend to examine with some care so that we may use instructional ministries among the saints intelligently and productively.

What's Going on Here Anyway?

Among Christians there is seldom much doubt or argument about *whether* we should study the Bible. We are constantly reminded that the Bible holds within its many books and special chapters the key to faith, life, and eternal salvation. To the vast majority of committed and well-meaning believers that is convincing enough on its own terms and sufficient cause to keep Bible classes, if not actually overcrowded, at least predictably steady in attendance, thus warranting continuing organization and scheduling.

Further, there are undeniably attractive inducements beyond the faith-building and equipping elements inherent in Biblical study. In a literary as well as literal sense studying the Bible is a fascinating adventure into an almost limitless treasure-house of poetry, wisdom, and history, where one gripping scenario after another is capable of stirring and inspiring us. Thus, we find ourselves confronting a situation of unquestioned merit, one that stands ever ready to support and help us, and finally, one that is both accepted and embedded in parish life.

So what is the problem? Since there is no apparent quarrel over *whether* the Bible should be studied, we should get on with it and worry about more pressing problems. Right? Not quite. Consider another aspect of the same situation. *How* should Christians be led in their study in adult Bible class settings? Posing this question suggests that effective study in the Bible class setting is dependent not only on knowledgeable leaders, but on differing ways and means to acquire knowledge, learn skills, and in general, sharpen up our Biblical expertise.

Those of us who have been through the mill as leaders and participants begin to recognize that at this point some uneasiness may begin to stir. In fact, if my hunch is on target, I just might be correct in assuming that something about our experience in Bible class study suggests quite strongly that it could be much better if only . . . And the *if only* sums up those unknown frustrations or misgivings, or even the shortcomings, we have ourselves recognized.

If there is to be a class, and if study is going to be involved, a few additional questions might be in order. What kind of a course or class is this? What kind of learning is supposed to take place? What kind of tools are we working with? Is the setting conducive to Bible *study?* Are the activities in the Bible class designed to enhance active learning and personal involvement? Or are the members more apt to be dependent listeners and passive learners? Can practical use be made of what is being studied? What difference will be made in the lives of the learners as a result of study?

Tough questions with no easy answers. But one thing is certain: the answers will give pointed indications about the strengths or weaknesses of the organization, leadership, and conduct of the parish Bible class.

Of course, there are a number of important factors that contribute to the success or failure of the typical Bible class program. *The issue raised in these pages focuses on but one of these many factors:* teaching and learning through the use of appropriate methods in adult Bible class settings.

Although such a study may contribute an answer or two to some of the problems posed above, it cannot address them all. But the contention at the outset is that the *how* of leading and participating in Bible class study can make or break the endeavor. In searching out the how, we hope to discover that these ways and means will involve Christian adults purposefully and meaningfully, thereby sketching out helpful tips for those who are on the participating or learning end of things.

Before coming to grips with these ways and means, however, there is a prior and equally important consideration. It necessarily precedes any selection of method. Unfortunately, this consideration, which focuses on how Christian adults are apt to learn most effectively, is usually given little, or only cursory, attention. More's the pity. As might be expected, this, too, has its consequences.

While not all failures can be traced to the disregard, neglect, or even disdain of those unique ways in which adults pattern their learning habits, it can at least be said that substantial progress has been unnecessarily blunted by leaders and participants who labor on at odds with the very basic dos and don'ts in this respect, thus undercutting potential achievement. Most of us are all too familiar with the problems. They have even been stereotyped and caricatured across denominations, featuring lecturing pedagogues; uninterested, even bored, participants;

and skimpy, if not negligible, results. Harsh? Perhaps—but in many cases regrettably true.

Stated in more positive terms from the perspective of potential benefit, we might suggest that *what* we know about the dynamics of adult learning ought to provide a solid base for the selection of appropriate means for productive Bible study. If we know something about the condition and potential of the adult Christian learner we should be in a position to select methods that are consistent with the goals we have established for Bible study. It is indeed an awareness of all these factors *as* planning is done that enables us to take the proper steps to assure that something beyond sociability, as beneficial as that may be, can and will take place.

2

Some Fundamentals
Basics in Adult Christian Education

What, then, are some of these necessary considerations that undergird adult Christian education? From among the many provided by researchers and practitioners and from professionals in the field, these may be suggested as top priority items:

1. Redeemed Christians are special people. Claimed by God, they are regenerated beings with an astonishing variety of potentials. Prompted by God's Spirit, they are called to rise above their infirmities and sin as they begin to use effectively those gifts and talents they possess in the service of God and their neighbor. Those kind of people live for others, and because they are blessed with the special gifts that Christ has made possible through His death and resurrection, they are led to know and believe that theirs is a special responsibility, a special mission, that of building Christ's Body, the church.

2. Because they are in fact God's people, adults learn from His Word. They have both the need and desire to come to grips with the tasks, responsibilities, problems, and daily situations stemming directly from their involvement in the mission of the church. Their primary source for direction, wisdom, and strength *is* God's Word. That is precisely what makes Bible *study* such a fundamental essential in the life and growth of the church.

3. One of the most powerful variables at work in adult learning situations is individual and collective experience. When the past experiences of the learners are tapped as contact points with learning, it is a pretty sure bet that something noteworthy or significant is going to happen.

4. Adult Christians are motivated to learn in areas related to current responsibilities and particularly during times of concern, crisis, or transition. For the past several years, much of the pop, as well as scholarly, literature about learning on the adult level has emphasized again and again the crucial nature of transitions from one stage of adulthood to another, or of the passing from one status or role in life to another. At such times it is not only information that is needed. Skills, expertise, understanding, and compassion are in demand. They are all needed to overcome some of those tough problems we face or to help us cope with the stress and setbacks of daily living. As the old commercial suggested, it can be a real jungle out there and we need all the help we can get. To make the point: these kinds of situations are made to order for high level, productive, and satisfying learning. Furthermore, they present us with opportunities to minister to one another both near and far.

5. New information, changes, or new responsibilities often threaten adults, not only in life, but in the class setting as well. Anxiety or outright stress at such times is reduced by providing time to talk things over and to discover ways and means to take positive, helpful action.

6. Timing, health, obstacles of one kind or another, and the pressures of that continuing struggle with "the daily dozen" influence our potential and our effectiveness in dealing with these learning situations. When, how long, how much it will take in terms of personal investment, or whether we feel it will really be worth the effort; these and other seemingly unimportant considerations often color the situation more than most class organizers and teachers are ready to admit—or even understand.

7. Christian adults usually come to the learning situation with some deep inner convictions. They have a number of cherished, often privately held goals, and, although they may not share them, they also have strong ideas about what is for them actually useful subject matter. In fact, some of the traits scholars and teachers treasure most, like verbal artistry, the gathering of tons of information, reasoning capabilities, or even a facility with abstract ideas, can be real turn-offs for some adults.

8. In volunteer learning programs, like the adult Bible class, the practicability and useful transfer of the learning is a virtual must. The more time spent on piling up facts for the sake of piling up facts the sooner the point of no return is reached, and with it, lost interest and unfulfilled goals.

Among other factors vieing for consideration, these eight, then, have been singled out as especially noteworthy. Figure 1 presents some of the implications inherent in these variables. Perhaps your experience or further thought will provide still more. Ultimately, these implications should guide both design and practice in adult Bible classes.

FIGURE 1 Instructional Principles and Their Implications for Adult Christian Education

Principle	Implication for adult Christian education
1. God's redeemed are special people.	The redeemed and reconciled nature of the relationship between God and His people is the foundation on which adult Christian education is premised. It places Jesus Christ at the heart and core of all educational endeavor. The gospel empowers adult Christians to use God's gifts in ministry.
2. God's special people, adult Christians involved in ministry, rely on the Bible for counsel, aid, and comfort.	God's Word is the primary source, norm, and guide for daily living, for assuming responsibilities, solving problems, and for directing our relationships with others as well as with our Lord and Savior. God's Spirit, moving in us through that Word, enables us to accept and to learn about our responsibilities as Christians in this world, and with an assured hope and conviction about the world to come.
3. The past experience of the learners is a vital ingredient in learning at the adult level.	When our past spiritual, social, vocational, or family experiences are related to information or activities in learning, we are more inclined to incorporate the learning effectively into the structure of daily living and of Kingdom building. Necessary starting points in educational settings include both the Word and interpersonal relationships based on some knowledge of the learners, so that timely information and insight may be brought to bear on teaching and learning.
4. A powerful motivation to learn occurs when adults experience life-transitions or a crisis.	The planning of educational programs should take into consideration the various life-stages and life-transitions experienced by Christian adults. Potential, predictable, or actual crises provide similar challenges. Marital, family, vocational, social, or spiritual considerations provide background and opportunity for relating information, expertise, skills, and understanding based on the Word in timely and compassionate settings where these predictable situations are either dealt with, or prepared for.
5. New information, or change, or new responsibilities are often perceived by adults as threatening, and thus inhibiting to learning.	Christian teachers and discussion leaders will want to control tension so that it can be used as a positive factor in learning by (a) identifying, analyzing, and clarifying troublesome situations or problems; (b) by defining the kinds of action or conduct necessary to achieve desired outcomes; and (c) by providing for response or reactions without the fear of failure or reprisal on the part of the participants.
6. Adult Christians tend to learn most effectively when their physical and mental capacities are equal to the task and when they are provided with sufficient time and appropriate facilities.	Scheduled events should realistically account for the amount of time learners are willing to invest. Provision for appropriate sight, sound, and other physical facilities are major factors in the success or failure of adult programs. Supportive assists, quality materials and equipment, and sufficient facilities go a long way toward assuring success in educational programming.
7. The skills, priorities, and goals of the learners often differ radically from those of program planners or instructional personnel.	Successful programs of adult Christian education will not be based only on content or the kind of skill development deemed necessary by practitioners or even the unique personalities of instructors. An equally strong consideration is the process of determining the learning goals, and this is the point at which the learners must be taken into consideration so that they may be meaningfully involved at levels of performance that are challenging to them, while yet capable of achievement.
8. For adults one of the highest priority items in education and training is the practicability and useful transfer of learning.	The New Testament repeatedly accents the equipping of the saints, a feature that anticipates the need to instruct Christian adults purposefully, with an eye toward the daily practice of skills and attitudes capable of building Christ's Body, the church (see the following passages: Eph. 4:4–13; II Tim. 3:10–17; Heb. 10:23–25). Adults tend to want what they learn to be useful. Their preferences lie in useful and practical training. Successful administrators and teachers have understood that basic feature and organized instruction accordingly.

To summarize the main points of these preliminary considerations:

1. Personal Bible study, congregational Bible classes, and
extra-congregational Bible study programs have been and will
remain basic to adult Christian education.

2. Bible study should be organized and conducted on the
basis of known and shared principles capable of guiding the
endeavor so that it will proceed effectively, not only for the
adults involved, but toward the greater goal of building Christ's
Body, the church. That calls for a careful study of both the Bible
and the adult learner and, further, of the dynamics of the
learning and teaching process in adult Christian education
settings.

3. Such elements as the power of the gospel; our past
experiences, capabilities, needs, problems, and life-stages; and
the potential usefulness of the learning undertaken are all top
priority considerations in the approach to adult Christian education.

4. Having outlined the essential considerations at least in
broad strokes, I would further contend that the next order of
business is to find ways and means capable of producing not
only what is socially and popularly acceptable, but more
importantly, of achieving results in accord with the goals of
mission, ministry, and Kingdom building.[1]

5. The focus of attention in our search for possible ways and
means will, therefore, be on methods that foster Christian
fellowship, an understanding of Biblical knowledge and its
wisdom, and in particular, the development of the necessary
range of skills adult Christians call on daily to meet the
challenges of a faith-life active in love.

And so our attention is drawn to methods. That used to be
considered unnecessary because one method and only one
dominated educational activity—the combination of lecturing
and discussions based on a question-answer format. Aside from
an assist here or there from media, usually film (which is an
animated version of a lecture), the vast majority of teaching
featured the lecture. Not so any more. We finally seem to have
understood that, while this method is good for certain kinds of
learning, it is certainly not good for them all. But that raises the
question: What else is there? This has been a maddening and
highly provocative question in the recent past for Christian
educators, totally committed as they were to lecturing and
demonstrating styles.

1. The term, *"Kingdom building"* is used throughout these pages to indicate
all those activities suggested by the Scriptures; which, under God's hand and
blessing, build and sustain His church. Among those passages indicated, several
refer specifically to that part of *Kingdom building* that emphasizes the study of
the Word: Matt. 16:24–25; Luke 14:25–33; John 12:20–26; Acts 1–5; 17:10–15;
Gal. 5:16–6:10.

Perhaps if we are able to get at some of the reasons for doing what we are doing in adult Christian education, we will be in a better position to tailor the means to the goals we seek to achieve. To do that we will consider, from among a number of concerns, at least these: What does the method under consideration actually consist of? What are its strengths, weaknesses, prime capabilities? Is the method consistent with our understanding of the context, the dynamics of the teaching-learning process, the content, and the people in Christian education?

That points the way to an investigation focusing on method as a delivery system for educational process. Or put another way; we will put method under the microscope to see what makes it tick. Ultimately, having looked at method in general, we will take a closer look at several methodologies in particular, some of which hold promise as especially well suited to the rather unique requirements of the Bible class setting.

3

Ways and Means
A Look at Method

What will it take to get the job done? That is a question most practical-minded people want answered before getting on with the task at hand.

Pete, 8, and Erin, 10, were fishing off the pier at dusk one summer day and Pete was steaming. His older sister's bobber was going under so often and she was pulling up so many pan fish compared to his pitiful little handful, it was unbearable. To be outdone by your sis? What could be worse! It seemed to Pete as if a line had been drawn down the middle of the pier, and all the fish were on Erin's side. So Pete shuffled over to the other side, dropped his line, and waited to move in on the kill. Except that nothing changed. Erin pulled in a few more, and Pete came up empty-handed except for his mounting frustration. It ruined an otherwise perfect vacation day.

What would it have taken to get the job done? Better bait? Maybe Pete jerked his line around too much? The hook? Ah yes, the hook! Pete's was so tiny and bent out of shape that all it managed to do was feed the fish. His hook wouldn't have snared a minnow. It simply was not up to the task. Quite obviously, a better hook was needed to get the job done.

So too, with methods. Different kinds of learning or training or development call for different approaches. And that brings us to a question that must always be raised at the very outset: How can the goal be accomplished most effectively and with the most benefit to one and all? The answer will, without doubt, involve ways and means, or combinations of ways and means.

The problem of Pete's hook has been repeated over and over

in congregational education settings. Many classes organized for various church groupings and Bible classes rely almost exclusively on one method, or at most a very limited number, for all the training, study, and enrichment activities they offer. If it just so happens that the goal can be achieved through one of the methods in this limited arsenal, fortune may smile benignly, crowning the effort with success.

The time soon comes, however, when in the cold light of sober after-thought it may just occur that success, in the long run, has been spotty. And then the question, Why not such success regularly? At that point a searching look at all the variables begins, or at least should begin. There will be an examination of *the way* the job was done, for that will most assuredly have something to say about the outcome. And here concerns about method begin.

Factors in Selecting a Method

Method and Fellowship

While we are on the subject of fundamentals and basic starting points, we should note that we engage in these studies and classes together. It is a cooperative effort featuring a fellowship dimension that accents love, concern, and compassion among this bonded communion of believers. We are involved with one another; teachers and leaders with learners or trainees, and learners with one another. No one enrolled because of the grade, or even for a possible reward of money.

What we do together and the way we do it together aims at a higher goal, that of building one another up in the faith and for service in mission. In such a situation skill development and learning facts is undeniably important, but so also is our concern for community in Christ and the goals we seek to achieve as a communion of saints in mission. Consequently, the dynamics of the situation weigh heavily on our choice of methodology, which, in turn gives direction to our search for the kinds of methods capable of scholarly or skillful achievement while at the same time fostering, preserving, and even enhancing the dimension of fellowship. The first element of our investigation has focused on the relationship between methodology and the fellowship dimension that exists among leaders and learners.

Method and the Learner's Potential

Another consideration necessary in the selection of methods for teaching and learning at the adult level is the learner's nature and potential. Here, too, there is a strong relationship between our estimate of the adult's status and capabilities, under God, and the kinds of activities we select for instructional purposes. Methods are not neutral. They have the power to promote active learning, or to render the learner quite passive. If, for example, our attitude is positive and our expectations high, we will make it our business to select means consistent with an active approach to the learning objective, taking into consideration the past experience, current skills, or needs of the learner.

The learner is, and remains, in any case, the focal point of the learning situation. In selecting procedures for learning, therefore, the estimate of worth or potential or resource the instructor sees in the learner will be a factor in deciding on ways and means chosen to achieve desired goals.

Method and the Word

Still another consideration involves the Bible directly. We look to God's Word as the key source, the touchstone, as it were, against which all of the realities in this life and in that which is to come are measured. (Ps. 119:130–133) It has been suggested that each day's experience, for the Christian, is informed, guided, and judged by what the Scriptures say. It makes sense, then, for the methods we use in study and training programs to be capable of drawing us ever deeper into the Scriptural message. One of the most crucial considerations in this respect is the extent to which the learner is personally and intimately drawn into that message. Again, methods have a way of being less than neutral. We are all acquainted with classes that involve leaders intensely, quite intimately, with the scholarship of Biblical study, while the learners have been more or less sidelined by a one-way conversation *about* the Bible that has somehow failed to get us *into* the Bible.

Method and Skill Development

A fourth concern of methodology has to do with its relationship to skill development. Is the method capable of providing for the development of skills? A prime example would be the skill of witnessing. Here is a responsibility, as well as privilege, that each Christian is called upon to demonstrate to all people, and especially to those outside the household of faith. The witnessing skill is but one of a staggering array implicit in the tasks of mission and ministry.

Naturally, we cannot expect that all methodologies will provide this skill, nor is the skill training dimension a necessary part of every study session. However, the continuing concern for effective ministry surely gives cause to provide regularly for skill training in our various programs of adult Christian education. When that time comes, it is the method that, to great extent, bears the burden of producing workmanlike results.

Method and Instructional Potential

Finally, and from a more instructional perspective, we are concerned about the method's potential for: (a) achieving stated learning, enrichment or training goals; (b) assisting in the development of our inner resources and God-given abilities; and (c) developing the necessary capabilities that enable us to cope with our lives as Christians.[1] This particular yardstick has to do with the organization, goal, and net results in the teaching and learning transaction.

Our list has grown to five of the more prominent factors in a consideration of the place and relationships involved in the selecting of methods for the education of Christian adults. Before moving on to a study of figure 2, which depicts a number of methodologies under the scrutiny of five basic concerns, it will be helpful to summarize them briefly.

1. Christian brothers and sisters in fellowship with one another and in Jesus Christ seek ways and means to learn, be trained, and be enriched that are consistent with the features and blessings of fellowship. (I John 1:5-7; Titus 3:14)
2. The nature of these Christian learners and of their potential as believers, and our understanding of that potential, gives direction to the selection of ways and means that will assist in attaining the goals of the learners.
3. The Bible is our primary text and we want to be involved in it knowledgeably, skillfully, and reverently. That makes a concern for method a strategic, essential factor. (Acts 17:11; James 1:19-25)
4. The skill dimension in ministry focuses on the capability of methods to prepare adult Christians for effective and active participation in the mission of the church. (1 Chron. 16:8-36; Acts 1:1-8; Rom. 12:9-13)
5. The methods should serve strictly instructional purposes, such as the achievement of learning or training objectives; the enrichment and development of abilities and inner resources; and the training of skills necessary for coping with daily responsibilities *as* Christians. (Col. 2:6-10; 2 Peter 2:1-10)

---

1. You have probably noticed that *ability* and *capability* are deliberately used in different settings. That is because *ability* is used in the sense of God-given, innate gifts; *capability* is used in the sense of trained or developed *ability*. Thus, reasoning would be an ability, but the logical development of thought would be a capability.

Types of Method

Now that we have examined method in general from a number of rather specific perspectives, we are in a position to look at several methodologies in particular. Several of the more common styles, or types, are represented in figure 2. They are divided into two basic categories, the one featuring methods largely dependent on expository or presentation techniques, and the other, dependent on methods that may be characterized as exploratory or problem/learner-centered in nature. The figure analyzes these methods from the standpoint of the five concerns outlined above and for their potential overall for the several types of learning in which most Bible classes engage. In this latter respect, the cue for judgment is based on three factors, designated 1–2–3 in each instance, which represent potential capability for instruction in knowledge, skill development, and attitude.

From this mass of highly concentrated information (figure 2) we should be able to draw a number of significant conclusions. First, however, it might be helpful to call attention to the two groupings, or categories, into which these methods are divided. One has been designated *presentation types*. Further identification has been added by means of an additional word, *expository*. The other has been designated *exploratory*, and further identified with the words *problem/learner-centered*. Here we have two basic characterizations capable of gathering within the scope of their fundamental nature a number of methodologies or strategies. Let's take a closer look at these categories.

Presentation Types

A number of instructional characteristics fall neatly into place when the lecture, demonstration, panel, or forum are analyzed. For one thing, the teacher, or coordinator, will exercise decisive leadership to keep the teaching and learning situation in firm control. In these types of strategies control of the process is recognized by all involved as residing in the leader, or expert, as the case may be. Expertise is expected of those in charge, and a willingness to be informed or led is expected of the learners. In such situations the learners generally approach the learning task with limited knowledge and few skills to help achieve established goals.

Presentation methodologies are ideal to get the ball rolling. We simply can't expect to be in control when we are not knowledgeable or skilled in a given area. So, our initial attempts are made under the control of those who have assumed responsibility for guiding us. It is important, then, to have available a variety of means to accent the demonstration or impart dimension of instruction. At these early stages it is

Figure 2 **Presentation or Expository Types and Exploration or Problem/Learner-Centered Types**

Presentation or Expository Types

Method	Characteristic Features	The Biblical Concern	The Fellowship Concern	Learner Concerns	Skill Dimension Concern	Instructional Concerns	Potential Capacity to Teach — Knowledge (1), Skill (2), Attitude (3)
Lecture and speech types	A presentation of information, either live or by means of recording, tape, etc.	Great potential for scholarly attention to salient issues, thorough coverage.	Interaction is restricted through seating patterns and dominant position of speaker.	Limited concern except where speech is tailored specifically for a homogenous grouping.	Restricted to presenting a knowledge base for skills. Not suited to skill development.	Instructional goals achievement restricted. Inner Development limited. Development of coping skills limited.	(1) Excellent (2) Limited (3) Restricted effect; limited and short-range
Demonstration and laboratory types	These presentation types demonstrate an act or procedure. Ultimate intent is for viewer to become a performer.	Wise choice of demonstrable material may assist learners in acquiring Biblical expertise.	Restricted. Good on individual basis, fair to poor for group interaction.	High, to the extent that demonstration or laboratory exercise is within capabilities of learners.	Can be very helpful. High potential for mastery development.	Instructional goals achievement can be high. Inner development limited. Development of coping skills can be fair to good.	(1) Limited (2) Excellent (3) Limited
Panel, forum, and symposium types.	These types feature experts who present information on a given subject to groups.	Can be excellently accommodated. Organized and differentiated aspects of Biblical insight can be contributed by members.	Rather limited because listeners are directed by, and preoccupied with, the panels and their expertise.	Limited to the extent that the topic covers an expressed need at a given time.	Limited. Skills usually remain in possession of gathered experts.	Instructional goals achievement can be high. Inner development limited. Development of coping skills is quite limited.	(1) Excellent (2) Limited (3) Restricted
Programming and contracting types.	These types, along with packaged learning, present completely preorganized information, indicating procedures and expected outcomes.	Might be helpful under special circumstances for certain aspects of Biblical study.	Quite limited. Each learner occupied with personal efforts to proceed toward programmed objectives.	Can be very high depending on assessment of individual learner's ability and status.	Could be very satisfactory. One-to-one checkpoints monitor skill development skill development progression.	Great potential for achievement of instructional goals. Inner development often limited. Development of coping skills is fair.	(1) Very good (2) Fair to good (3) Limited

Exploration or Problem/Learner-Centered Types

Method	Characteristic Features	The Biblical Concern	The Fellowship Concern	Learner Concerns	Skill Dimension Concern	Instructional Concerns	Potential Capacity to Teach Knowledge (1) Skill (2) Attitude (3)
Institute and workshop types.	Under leadership of experts, groups work through problems, projects, or situations to gain directed experience or produce handiwork, research, etc.	Great potential for Biblical expertise, as well as application of product to parish life.	Somewhat limited, though provision for interaction on several levels would enhance fellowship possibilities.	To the extent that common interests prevail, this type has high potential to meet learner needs, objectives.	Excellent. These types are especially well suited to skill sharpening.	Instructional goals achievement is fair to good. Inner development is limited. Development of coping skills is good.	(1) Fair (2) Excellent (3) Fair to good
Seminar types.	Learners have direct and sustained access to experts in charge.	Excellent from a knowledge and insight standpoint. Directed study and research capability into topics or ethical problems on Biblical basis.	Probably weakest in the exploration category, but skillful leadership can modify the situation. Experts should not dominate.	Rather limited. Seminar types organized around stated learner needs or problems are most successful.	Research and organization of data are prime skills, and therefore limit usefulness.	Instructional goals achievement is limited. Inner development is fair to good. Development of coping skills is limited.	(1) Excellent (2) Limited (3) Restricted
Group discussion types.	Informal, though directed conversation-type discussions guided by leaders trained in topic areas.	Although the potential is high, achievement usually is not. Goals must be clearly known and diligently pursued.	Very high potential. Usually a situation of low threat. Learners interact frequently.	Potential for individual attention and group concern is high and usually achieved.	Less likely to be achieved unless leaders and learners are intent on achieving skill mastery.	Instructional goals achievement is good. Inner development can be rather high. Development of coping skills is fair to good.	(1) Fair to good (2) Restricted (3) Excellent
Case study and problem solving types.	Feature written or stated problem areas for analyzing, studying, and suggesting remedies or a course of action.	Bible abounds in case-study types and can be used as source for both problem and solution study.	Skillfully led, the fellowship concern is very high. Cooperative efforts build morale.	Dependent on intelligent selection of problems and case studies. Potential great for meeting learner's concerns, needs.	Skills must first be taught, *then* used in these types. This often frustrates the situation.	Instructional goals achievement is good. Inner development can be excellent. Development of coping skills can be excellent.	(1) Good (2) Good (3) Excellent

necessary to get the learners, as soon as practicable, into a position of knowledgeability as a basis for still further achievements in the area of problem solving and coping with the situations that daily confront us. *Presentations* of one kind or another serve that purpose well.

Exploration Types

There are different assumptions, dynamics, and aims at work in the methodologies grouped under *exploration* types. In the first place, assumptions are made about the learner that take into account some prior acquaintance with the material or skills under consideration. Further, the teacher, or expert, usually expects to know more about each learner and to foster more deliberately a caring, concerned spirit among the members. Leaders then begin to work *with*, instead of striving exclusively *for*, both knowledgeability and skills, bending them toward more pressing and demanding family, vocational, spiritual, or problem-solving situations.

Consequently, a premium is placed, not only on the acquisition and use of helpful skills, but also on attitude development and considerations of personal and group morale. Strategies featuring inquiry, discovery, cooperative endeavor, and a spirit conducive to an esprit de corps, are now called into use. A significant difference in the role of leadership can also be detected: the leader becomes more readily accessible, more closely associated with members, personal goals, and results. A subtle change from a potentially distant *you* to a more involved *we* prevails as all assume responsibilities on a more equal basis. Among adults that purpose, along with its procedural assumptions, is best served by case studies, workshop or institute types, discussion groups, and others that promote active participation in many of the aspects of the instructional setting.

The sampling of methodologies in figure 2 represents a selection of the more popular types most parish Bible class members have encountered. There are, of course, more. But it should also be pointed out that the eight types do represent about as many styles as are profitable for use. Many of the other strategies are actually techniques used as aids or resources rather than as methods or strategies per se. The skill of questioning or the use of supportive visuals come to mind in this connection.

Finally, what conclusions and inferences can we draw from this analysis (figure 2) of method, concern, and potentials? To start with, a pointed restatement: the two major method categories, presentation and exploration, and the strategies within them, each with unique capabilities and procedural nuances, are best suited for given purposes and possess the ability to produce rather predictable outcomes. For example, presentation methodologies are more restricted in scope while exploration methodologies are more versatile.

Taking these various items into consideration, we can readily see that it is necessary to assess the instructional task in terms of the context for learning, and of the makeup of the learning group, *and then* make strategy decisions that are appropriate to given needs or purposes. Let me tack that down with an example. In addressing a need for facts or a concentrated approach to a particular area of knowledge, lecturing will serve that purpose well. On the other hand, developing a skill in Biblical interpretation calls for a methodology in the exploration category, such as a series of skill-mastery sessions or perhaps a workshop setting.

One of the more critical class priorities has to do with exploring and, above all, encouraging positive attitudes about Bible study. And even beyond that, we definitely seek Biblical counsel for the responsibilities, conduct, and meaning of a faith-life anchored in Jesus Christ. Such an objective suggests settings and strategy selection that emphasize supportive interpersonal relationships. Further, it surely helps to be guided by perceptive, caring leaders.

In checking the possibilities there is persuasive evidence for selecting exploration types. Two of these, in particular, case studies and discussion groups, have proven to be consistently productive, especially when leaders and participants are alert to the potential, as well as dynamics of interaction inherent in these strategies.

We will surely want to keep in mind a factor repeatedly called to our attention by professional educators of adults: the participants' expectations, past experience, life-stage, and responsibilities, and similar considerations have profound effect on learning potential and on productivity. Therefore, our selection of strategies for the teaching and learning situation will favor the exploration types that accommodate such specific concerns.

In fact, the proportion of methodologies selected should, in the long term, weigh heavily in favor of these exploratory types precisely because of the nature and predominating expectation of the Bible class setting. And that pretty much lays bare one of the central contentions of this analysis of Bible class programming at the adult level: at least one of the reasons for spotty and sometimes discouraging results is a continuing reliance, if not stubborn insistence, on methodologies that are simply inadequate for achieving the goals set for learning and fellowship, particularly those that have to do with attitude and skill development. These are, at bottom, the real, or actual targets we aim for because they are fundamental to our determination and to our performance in daily living as believers.

Missing those targets causes us to admit, however sadly, that the program or class is, in the final analysis, irrelevant. Yet, on the other hand, how uplifting and encouraging to be able to point to examples of study programs in which the Bible has a telling effect on those involved because, through intelligent use of God-given ability and insight, concerns are addressed by His Word through ways and means that actively engage people in the search for solutions to problems, understanding and meaning, and comfort.

Such considerations quite clearly set presentation methodologies into the role of presenting information and mastering fundamentals which serve essential, albeit restricted, capacities. Thus, the instructional pattern comes clearly into view. We move from information gathering made available through lecturing and symposium strategies, and through other forms of presenting factual data, to the more complicated and challenging task of applying information knowledgeably, analyzing situations or problems, prioritizing our value structure as we face decisions, dilemmas, or problems. These concerns are at the heart of adult need and of adult nurture.

My purpose here has not been to downgrade one methodological type simply to favor another. The general categories we established have vital contributions to make in the churches' educational enterprise. Rather, the intent has been to develop these themes to the point where it might be possible to suggest that a series of from–to progressions is involved in this teaching and learning situation: from learning dependency to learning independency; from rather passive to appropriately active participation; and from leader-dominated presentation strategies to the problem- and peer-oriented, exploration types. (See also Appendix C.) We will examine both method types with a number of samplings ready-made for Bible class use, but our investigation emphasizes such strategies as the case-study and skill-mastery approaches to nurture because of their superior potential.

4

Summing Up and Looking Ahead

Up to this point the concerns in these initial chapters have, in one way or another, focused on teaching and learning in adult settings generally, and in Bible class settings in particular. Our primary aim, however, has been to narrow our focus gradually from a number of important variables down to one, training our sights specifically on methods and their potential for helping us accomplish something worthwhile in our study of the Scriptures.

We will not lose sight of each of these necessary considerations, but we will emphasize those factors in the two figures that analyzed some of the major instructional principles (figure 1) and a number of features inherent in different methodologies (figure 2). Two concerns might be singled out: (1) What, specifically, can a given method do? (2) What are the strengths and possible weaknesses of each method?

Having reviewed and determined the potential merits and shortcomings, we ought to be able to design a strategy for learning that will assist us in achieving our goals from the standpoint of both the learner and the teacher. Having been forewarned, we will be just a bit more selective about what we do and how we do it so as to derive the best possible benefit from the effort, time, and sacrifice we pour into this unique study situation, the Bible class.

And so we pause before moving on to a more detailed look at the three basic approaches in this study (lecture-discussion, skill mastery, and case-study approaches) to recap some of the more striking considerations raised. Basically, there are two general concerns:

I. Concerns about the Overall Rationale and Approach
   A. Different kinds of learning necessitate different teaching
      approaches, as well as different learning strategies.
   B. The goals to be achieved govern the choice of method,
      as well as the overall strategy governing the entire
      process.
   C. The unique demands of congregational Bible classes
      require that teachers and leaders choose ways and
      means to support and build up the special fellowship
      concerns we have come to cherish and expect, while at
      the same time accommodating the need for information
      and the skill dimension implicit in the mission and
      ministry of the church. (Rom. 15:1–7; Eph. 4:11–16;
      I Pet. 2:1–7).
   D. Since one of the major tasks in Christian teaching is to
      bring each learner into a real and personal encounter
      with the Word of God, we will want to make certain
      that the Scriptures are basic, primary sources, thus
      directing not only the choice of content, skill, or
      development of attitudes, but the instructional
      methodology as well. (John 17:13–20; Eph. 2:1–10; Heb.
      4:12–16).
   E. Because one of the prime purposes for any method or
      technique in Bible study programs is to bring the
      learner into an intimate relationship with Jesus Christ
      as Lord and Savior, we want to keep right on testing
      our methods to determine their effectiveness, especially
      regarding this personal relationship with Jesus Christ.
      (Titus 2:11–15; I John 4:1–7).
   F. The methods we choose should have the capability of
      ministering to the inner man so that through the Word,
      God's Spirit can and will affect and direct the adult
      saints from within. (John 16:5–16; Rom. 8:1–17).
   G. The choice of methodology should be governed by its
      capability for opening up the individual to active and
      collaborative participation, seeking to support and
      enrich the communion of saints. (I Cor. 1:4–9; 12:5–11;
      Eph. 4:7–8).
   H. There is comfort in knowing that a little of this and a
      little of that also has its proper place in the selection of
      methods. Variety, change of pace, novelty, and
      well-timed doses of the tried and true are all part and
      parcel of effective programming, strategy, and teaching.
II. Concerns about Instructional Progression
   A. Presentation strategies are best suited for the initial
      stages of an educational sequence, when we find
      ourselves in need of information, insight, and
      understanding that will set the stage for personal
      knowledgeability and the achievement of goals in the

mission and ministry of the church. Demonstrations, films, lectures, panels, etc., all serve this purpose admirably. They provide us with organized material and a common base of information that will position us to achieve our goals purposefully and effectively.

B. Exploration strategies are best suited for advanced stages of development. They enable us to work as active and contributing individuals toward either personal or corporate goals. Such strategies presuppose that the basics are in place and ready to be used as we move on to more active participation. This scenario usually involves skill development, workshop, case-study, or other involvement strategies to good advantage.

C. Limitations are implicit both in what has just been said and by what has been left unsaid. The most obvious conclusion is that presentation and exploration methods cannot hope to achieve substantial results either exclusively, or for each other. That suggests that each educational program or course, if you will, has its own rate of progression from one methodology to the other. Invariably the procedure will be from presentation to exploration.

To cap this summary here are a few implications. First and rather obviously, both presentation and exploration strategies have their proper and legitimate place in any educational endeavor. At times one will be more prominent than the other. It should be noted, however, that both can be effective, given the right goals, situation, and necessities. And, as you are surely able to guess, the trouble arises from an insistence that one or another can or must do all things and be used under all circumstances. That is precisely the point at which most Bible classes founder.

Another implication, especially for the learner, would be that he has a right to expect that the course of study be tailored, at least to some extent, to personal and group needs so that the instruction will in fact be effective, moving from the more passive initial stages to directed involvement. It stands to reason that without attention to the capabilities and needs of the learners, instruction will miss the mark. In that case the leader can only hope to move the enterprise along by appealing to a number of general considerations or challenges for future action. Speaking for those who are on the taking end, my earnest request would be for the teacher, expert, or professional to hit the learner where it counts. Get on my wavelength, please, and jar a few exposed nerve endings for a change.

Learning for the sake of learning has its proper place, but it is not yet the ultimate end of every educational program. God expects us to be active workers and witnesses in His vineyard.

Just one straightforward reminder from His Word: "We are his workmanship, created in Christ Jesus for good works, which God prepared beforehand, that we should walk in them." (Eph. 2:10) Heeding such a call places us in a position that calls for the kinds of skills, as well as information and outlook, that will enable us, with His help, to succeed. This suggests that our study sessions should be a basis for moving out into purposeful and informed ministry and not merely platforms for well-reasoned, clever, or entertaining performances. Giving the arts-for-arts-sake its just due, there is beyond that point a call to action that quite obviously necessitates a full range of equipping activity.

What follows, then, is a careful examination of several ways and means to accomplish these purposes. We are going to search out the component parts, analyze them, take them apart, and put them back together, as it were, so that we will know just what to expect and how we can use each to best advantage.

Part

That Old Standby Lecture-Discussion

The description, analyses, and examples of strategies that follow are singled out for investigation because they are either widely and popularly used, as in the case of the lecture-discussion lessons outlined, or because their instructional potential commends them highly as versatile, yet effective. They are, by every instructional standard on the adult level, well suited, not only for adult education, but for the singular demands of the Bible class setting. Examples given as worthy of consideration in this respect are skill mastery and case study, each represented by a number of instructional outlines.

Although the lecture has been treated previously as a presentation strategy, it will be noted that the examples given are actually organized on a lecture-discussion basis to meet such needs as fellowship, involved and active learning, and the development of independence on the part of the adult learners. Inherent in the lecture-discussion then, is a potential for tapping the best features of both styles. An additional reference, to a lecture per se, is provided in Appendix A. This lecture, presented to a pastoral conference, was intended primarily for instructional purposes, and is provided as a sampling of one approach and style lecturers may use as they seek to tailor the lecture to a given situation.

In the treatment of skill mastery and case studies, a number of examples are provided. Although some adaptations may be necessary to meet individual or local situations, these outlines are intended for use as presented.

5

The Lecture
Characteristics, Strengths, and Limitations

The lecture is by definition a presentation method because it imparts or presents information in the form of a speech to the audience. Such skills as identifying problems and addressing them or analyzing and organizing information are essential in preparing a lucid and interesting lecture. But it is not only important to be able to organize material and write well, the lecturer is further called upon to deliver his information clearly, understandably, and in a straightforward, well-enunciated style.

Characteristics and Procedures

Great speeches and outstanding speakers command our attention. They not only share common characteristics, but also tend to shape our expectations. The best of them hold us spellbound. Most of us have been exposed to a wide variety of lecture types and speaking styles in educational settings and community settings. So our examination of its characteristics will be confined to a limited number of the more salient issues of particular interest in the class situation.

As has been observed about the rose, so might we note that the lecture is a lecture is a lecture. We ought not be deceived by informal or even designed settings that seem to indicate we are all going to be an active part of the proceedings. Lecturers, at least those who are confirmed "speechers," surely are not fooled by the designs of those who might envision things otherwise. You are going to get your lecture come what may.

Having said that, we should note, however, that when it comes to presenting information in an economical and well-organized way, when we need to have a problem identified or a solution suggested, or indeed, if it is necessary to persuade or to approach a controversial issue, the lecture presents us with an ideal initial strategy.

In order for the lecture to succeed these considerations are basic:

1. The lecturer should be in a dominant, commanding position at a stage or platform elevation. Good lighting on the speaker and diffused lighting on the audience enhances both the speaker and the powers of concentration necessary for effective listening.
2. Introductions and conclusions by organizers or hosts are always in order. If the lecturer is known by all, as in the case of a dignitary or a local pastor, these courtesies are often omitted, though they are never out of place and most always give substantial support and significance to the situation.
3. The audience should work with supportive facilities that most enable them to follow the lecture meaningfully. Toward that end there should be sufficient lighting, perhaps an outline to follow, and writing surfaces for the purpose of taking notes.
4. The setting and circulation of air are two important factors. A pleasing and inspiring environment enriches the lecture immeasureably. An appropriately controlled climate and temperature are equally vital. Especially in smaller facilities, the massing of many people in confined areas takes oxygen and promotes a drowsiness that can be just as counterproductive as a monotone.

It may be objected that these circumstances seem to imply an elaborate, well-equipped facility. If that *is* the case in your local situation, there sould be no undue concern in preparing the setting but *do make certain* the lecture and the lecturer are given every chance to succeed. If forced by circumstances to present the lectures in smaller areas, they should not be allowed to alter the basic design and conditions for a presentation that counts for something. The smaller facility does need careful attention and more deliberate planning. This ultimately plays into the overall success of the Bible class scenario that features lectures on various topics or books of the Bible. The idea is that a lecture should be set up for its strengths and most productive purposes. That is surely not out of the reach or mind-set of parish planners or participants.

Strengths and Advantages

The strengths and advantages of lecturing can be summarized in two major considerations: the skill of the lecturer and the timeliness and applicability of the subject under consideration. There is not much doubt that a skilled, engaging lecturer can indeed hold the attention and interest of an audience. Add to that a particularly captivating topic and *viola!* the stage is set for *the* event. Under such circumstances the major strengths can become great advantages provided the purpose is appropriate for the outcome lecturing and follow-up discussion will produce.

These advantages include an organized perspective on the information being treated; delivering the information to many in succinct, clear, and stimulating fashion; and sharing the benefit of scholarly investigation that will enhance the understanding of many simultaneously. Attention to detail and planning is essential for success in the lecturing situation.

The foremost limitation of the lecture as an instructional method, particularly in such a setting as the Bible class, is its inability to generate meaningful exchange among members, or between individuals and the lecturer for that matter. Interpersonal relationships usually suffer because the content is given premium consideration at the expense of interaction and the flow of possible alternatives arising from the audience. The tipoff here is that most Bible classes make provision for discussion periods, however brief, to accommodate at least a few inquiries following the lecture. That arrangement openly acknowledges the need for inquiry and interaction on the issues raised that cannot be met by lecturing alone. Because we feel somehow unfulfilled unless that opportunity is provided, we have come to accept a combination of strategies as a standard operational procedure for many Bible classes in Christendom. The most frequent combination consists of lecture and guided discussion, often called simply the lecture-discussion method. Although that is an effective adjustment (or shall we call it a compromise?), it nonetheless underscores the point.

Other limitations include difficulties in achieving skill and attitude goals. Despite the objections of those who would use the lecture as a method for all seasons, the range of actual skill performance during a lecture is severely limited, at least for the hearers. Development of thought, note taking, and making mental record of cleverly turned phrases is about the sum of it. And as for the attitude dimension, there is rarely enough positive after-effect to stretch on into continued application and scholarly attention on a sustained basis. This is one of the prime reasons that repeated pleas from the pulpit, despite their eloquence, rarely produce the increased numbers in Bible classes urged upon the congregation. Those who are so inclined will be there anyway, and the rest furnish proof positive that this part of the sermon has apparently fallen on deaf ears.

Finally, it is well to remember that those who make up the audience usually bring dissimilar needs, capabilities, or interests to the Bible class lecture session. That being the case, individual concerns are necessarily subordinated. If it should so happen that most or all actually are at the same point and seek the same information, a lecture would, of course, be an excellent choice for an approach to the situation.

This brings to mind the advice passed on by a grizzled veteran of the old Chautauqua lecture circuit to a promising young scholar who envisioned himself as one of the famed lecturers on the circuit. Said the wise old pundit: "You're going to discover that there will be those who are determined to challenge you. Your first impulse will be to put those people in their place and silence them. But think twice before you do. They are probably among the few who had the patience to listen!"

Still another angle on the same theme is brought home by the incident in which the pastor lectured his Bible class on some difficult passages in Genesis. This latter-day Jonathan Edwards went on and on, finally putting the finishing touches on a tightly reasoned, information-packed lecture with, "Having looked at all the possibilities, what more can I say?" That was all the head elder needed to hear. His response was immediate and to the point, "Amen!" Both incidents carry their punch and you need no lecture to take note of the warning in each.

Participation Pointers

Many of us thrive on good lectures and attend them regularly. To the extent that participation is possible as we listen actively, we have no doubt developed personalized listening styles and a few additional tricks to help remember and benefit by what we have heard. Among the topmost skills are careful listening and sustained, determined concentration. The pointers are few, but important, as it turns out.

If the lecture topic is known in advance, a little preliminary research and study on the topic will go a long way in providing background and a point of comparison regarding the issues addressed by the lecturer. During the lecture a few notes at critical points, usually emphasized or repeated, will assist in getting at the thrust and meaning. An additional note or two relating an issue raised to personal experience will also prove beneficial. For those who do not take notes, it is important to concentrate on the flow of the lecture. It helps, too, to make a special mental effort to get down the three to four major points and rehearse them from time to time as the lecturer moves along. Usually, the speaker will provide enough strong hints or guideposts en route to point to issues worth remembering and examining. Finally, while the whole experience is still fresh in mind, the effort expended on follow-up study usually pays worthy dividends.

All Things Considered

The lecture method is much like a dangerous golf course that challenges the skills of determined golfers with bending fairways, menacing sandtraps, and tricky greens. Such a course has to be played carefully, with much respect and intense concentration. But that does not mean its challenge is insurmountable or that it will necessarily ruin the game for those who accept its challenge. So, too, with the lecture. With careful preparation that takes into account its weaknesses—avoiding them studiously—and its strengths—accenting them positively—the challenge of using this strategy can be met effectively and successfully.

If we can just overcome our almost total reliance on the lecture to accomplish every and any purpose envisioned for Bible study and use it only when its strengths match the purposes proposed, we will have covered a good piece of road in revitalizing the entire adult education program of the church. The foremost beneficiaries of that improvement would quite naturally be the Bible class program—along with all those patient saints in it.

Introduction to Strategy

The lecture-discussion combination frequently used in the Bible class setting may be developed in a number of ways. The lecture itself is, of course, the pivot point of the session in which the main themes are developed and explained. Audience participation takes the form of reaction and response, as well as answers to questions. Introducing, organizing, or clarifying new material or issues, and the review of old (hopefully relevant and historically significant material) or necessary information, is the major intent of the lecture, as well as of the ensuing discussion.

An approach to the actual layout of the lecture that most pastors will recognize is through their sermon writing skills. The sermon, after all, is a lecture, so one would expect that the organization and development of material, specifically tailored to the circumstances of the Bible class, would serve well. They know, and we too are aware that a well-written sermon, artistically delivered, is one of the finest and most frequently encountered examples of lecturing. Sermonic studies, therefore, are excellent material for the Bible class lecture.

Two such sermonic studies, with notes, are included in this study of strategies for the Bible class—and two only. Like the long sermon, which leaves us all uncomfortable, I do not want to run the risk of overkill, so we assume that the point has registered by the time the second of these two excellent studies has passed in review. Introductory material in the form of information about setting and learners, the theme, and an outline follow in each study.

Lecture-Discussion Outline I

Discipleship Demands Dedication [1]

Setting and Learners

On the basis of a good deal of experience with Bible class settings we are going to make a number of assumptions that will help identify and describe a rather typical class setting and its participants who, in this case, want to learn more about discipleship. Although many churches still use the nave for class sessions, a good number of congregations today have moved on to the more informal and congenial surroundings of education centers or meeting rooms of various sizes. That may be suitable for other strategies, but in the case of a lecture, the nave of the church may still serve best.

Some of the advantages of the larger gathering place, such as the main worship center, include these:

1. The listeners face the lecturer.
2. The lecturer is usually provided with a stand, lectern, or platform table, and in some cases with a microphone.
3. The gathering place usually is equipped with lighting that can be regulated.
4. In some cases, where pews have racks attached, mini-clipboards are provided as supports for those who may want to take notes.
5. Other facilities such as screens, projectors, etc., are easily accommodated and in most cases provided.

1. Adapted from a sermonic study prepared by Henry J. Eggold for the *Concordia Theological Monthly*, vol. 41, no. 3, (July 1977): 59–60.

The Achilles' tendon in this setting is, of course, the restriction placed on potential interaction. Architectural, as well as psychological, inhibitions very much limit the possibilities. Therefore, we shall assume that our lecture-discussion session will take place in an appropriate setting, provided with the kinds of facilities and Bibles (in sufficient numbers) that will enable us to profit from the lecture and to engage in a meaningful discussion.

Materials needed for this session are also assumed to be in plentiful supply, including an outline of the lecture for each participant. A lecture outline is an excellent aid to learning. It furnishes a well-organized progression of thought and provides space for additional notations.

The participants? A typical grouping would be composed largely of thirty to sixty-five-year-olds. However, it is commonplace to encounter study groups that consist of a smattering of people across a full spectrum of ages, representing a widely varied range of vocational and economic backgrounds. Finally, we shall assume that the lecture is to be given in a room spacious enough to accommodate seventy-five people arranged in a horseshoe around the focal point of the lecturer.

Lesson Theme and Its Biblical Basis

The theme, discipleship demands dedication, is taken from a sermonic study based on Luke 9:51-62.

Lesson Outline

Occasion and Continuity

This study of discipleship is to be the first in a series of five sessions devoted to the basis, requirements, and involvement of Christians committed to following the Savior. Most of the participants need a solid knowledge base before any of the skills of discipleship can be undertaken. Therefore, this series will be initiated with a lecture-discussion session aimed at inspiring the membership, as well as being informative. This Lukan account of events following Christ's transfiguration is an excellent choice for the opening session of a series.

Goals

1. Information about discipleship will be presented by means of the lecture based on Luke 9:51-62. Their study will be accommodated by an outline featuring: (a) Jesus' example of discipleship for us; and (b) the dedication required of His followers who would be His disciples.

2. Major issues will be discussed in the time provided, according to discussion groups and their appointed leaders.

3. Participants will summarize their findings, listing appropriate goals for future sessions and making individual application to their own situations by recording at least two discipleship goals for the coming week, with the understanding that time will be set aside in the next session for comparison of experiences based on a sharing of the discipleship goals.

Instructional Plan

I. Background Information and Commentary

Verse 51: This was not Jesus' last journey to Jerusalem, but one which would settle His fate as far as the Jews were concerned. "Received up": This points to the Ascension, with the passion and Resurrection intervening. *v. 52:* The Samaritans were a racially mixed people who accepted only the Pentateuch. There was little love lost between Jews and Samaritans (John 4:9). The Samaritans refused Jesus lodging. *v. 54:* "As Elias did" (Cf. I Kings 1:10). This is a doubtful reading. James and John, Sons of Thunder, had to learn the full lesson of humility. Christ was bent, not on destroying, but on saving souls. The Christian church does not use force in bringing the gospel to people. *v. 56:* "The Son of man is come." *v. 57:* Here are three would-be disciples. They evidence inconsiderate impulse, conflicting duties, and the divided mind. True discipleship implies denial of self and all earthly ties for the sake of the Kingdom. The first man did not count the cost of discipleship. *v. 59:* Jesus asks the scribe to become His disciple. "Let the dead bury the dead," i.e., Let those whose occupation it is, bury the dead. The need of preaching the gospel must take precedence over family duties. *v. 62:* "No man, having put his hand to the plow," i.e., He who would plow straight furrows must not look back. Following Jesus requires a firm intention and a steady eye. A person must devote his entire life to discipleship.

Introductory summary: Life demands dedication, the student to his studies, the businessman to his business, the housewife to her important work of childrearing. Discipleship, too, demands dedication.

Comment

Prior to the first session it would be advantageous for the participants to have at least these notes on background material, and even more beneficial to have, with it, a partial outline of the lecture.

Here are keys to major issues and discussion points for small group consideration.

II. Lesson Sequence

  A. Pre-session fellowship

  B. Opening devotion (leader) based on Luke 9:51–62

    Duration—5 minutes

  C. Introduction of speaker—(leader)

    Duration—2 minutes

  D. The Lecture

    Lecture Outline

This is a chronological sequence with provision for a 75 minute session, blocked out in sequential time allotments.

1. **Exemplified by Jesus**
   a) Jesus was on His way to Jerusalem.
   b) Jesus rebukes the disciples.
      From the purpose of saving the world Jesus did not falter.
      Never has anyone lived so dedicated a life.

Major points of the outline are presented. The prepared outline handout will provide space between headings for notations, inquiries, discussion suggestions.

2.   **Christ looks for dedication in us**
   a) Do not be rash. It takes dedication to be a Christian.
   b) Do not let important things keep you from the most important. Be dedicated. Some people always have something to do before being a disciple, Psalm 95:7. Christians sometimes major in minors.
   c) Do not let worldly things keep you from following Christ. The measure of a man is that in which he is dedicated. Put Christ first in your life, Matthew 22:37; 6:33.

   Duration, D—up to 15 minutes

This sermonic lecture is divided into two parts, easily remembered: Christ is an example for dedication, and Christ looks for dedication in His disciples. This theme should be emphasized so that those who are not note-takers will be able to participate in discussion groups effectively.

III. Discussion Starters (Leader)
   A. Questions, clarification of terms, observations, review of concepts

This part of the lesson sequence aims at understanding, a necessary and prior step to group discussions.

   B. Assignment of discussion groups, leaders, and designated discussion areas

   Duration, III—7–8 minutes
   BREAK

Prearranged leaders, prepared for special groupings, and color-coded ID markers will expedite assignments.

IV. Small Group Discussions (Assigned Group Leaders)
   A. Division into 8, fairly even-sized groups. Assignment: return to plenary session prepared to share two major issues or discussion points.

   Duration—up to 18 minutes.

Guided discussions in an informal, circular setting. Each leader prepared with several leading questions to assist flow of discussion.

V. Reassembly for Plenary Discussion (Leader)
   Brief report and reaction time for each of the discussion groups, general discussion.

   Duration—up to 13 minutes

Leadership is a key to good plenary meeting and meaningful discussion. Lecturer will serve as resource to discussion.

VI. Personal Challenge (Lecturer)
   Acting on conviction, conclusions in the week ahead. Taking the experience into life.

   Duration—2-3 minutes

The challenge arises from goal 3, selecting and acting on 2 discipleship goals during the coming week.

VII. Preview and Closing (Leader)

    A. Reminder of time, date, and topics for Session II; review of personal challenge.

    B. Closing Devotion

    Duration, VII—3-4 minutes

    Time elapsed for session: ca. 75 minutes

> The wrap-up and look ahead. Continuity develops with review and preview.

A Final Observation

The lecture-discussion lesson developed under the theme of Discipleship Demands Dedication has turned out to be a bit involved, taking us beyond the point of simplified arrangements and straightforward lecturing. Here we have an example of combined, synchronized elements at work. The essential centerpiece is the lecture, to be sure. But in this setting the lecture is used as a staging ground for a challenging discussion for those inclined to participate.

Through a series of tightly organized events, each with its own requirements and unique skills, and each with its own restrictions on time, a large group of people is provided an opportunity to be part of both listening and one-on-one situations. It has great potential for achieving some of the overarching goals each Bible class seeks: building one another up in the faith, and purposeful determination to build Christ's kingdom.

From an instructional standpoint such a combination can more readily achieve its goal of significant learning and attitude development than can the one-dimensioned lecture. That makes preliminary meetings, organization, preparation of materials, and those last-minute phone calls worth the effort. But then, real productivity, no matter the arena, is its own most demanding taskmaster, isn't it?

7

Lecture-Discussion Outline II

Making Mercy a Way of Life

This lecture-discussion study is developed for the many, many Bible classes that meet on Sunday mornings with an established time limit of one hour. Another restriction is that of number. In groups of twenty to forty people—the number envisioned for this study is thirty—there is a distinctly different dynamic at work than that of the setting in the previous study in which seventy-five were in attendance. It is not only time or numbers, however, that affect the organization of Bible class activity. In this particular session the lecturer is also the discussion leader. So the pace, direction, and flow of interpersonal activity is controlled by one, central, up-front figure. That is rather standard fare in most smaller congregations, and in many of the larger ones, as well. Consequently, this lesson will contrast with the previous one in a number of significant ways although the basics of the lecture-discussion methodology will be observed in the plan and sequence of the lesson.

Of special note will be the use of leadership and enabling skills on the part of the leader. These skills must, above all else, be wisely used so that discussions and interaction will not be conducted at a trivial and meaningless level. One of these skills, questioning, is used as the prime initiating point for group discussion and interaction. This art is further detailed in Appendix B.

Setting and Learners

This Bible class meets in a carpeted, spacious meeting room that is nicely appointed and amply supplied for discussion purposes. Equipment such as projectors and screens (an overhead projector is used in the sequence) is available. The study group members know one another well and have been served by their present pastor, who is also their Bible class leader, for a number of years. There is an easy informality about the membership.

Such a setting should sound familiar because it is so typical across denominations. And it is precisely the kind of setting that calls for constant attention and evaluation, because of the familiarity and engrained habits that tend to dull vitality and intensity. All the more reason to use lecture-discussion with utmost care, and as a change-of-pace, rather than routinely as a strategy for Bible class study.

Lesson Theme and Its Biblical Basis

Making Mercy a Way of Life is the theme. It is based on a dual selection from Luke 13:10-17 and I Corinthians 9:19–23. The background information is adapted from one of the specially prepared series of adult lessons by James Reapsome.[1]

Lesson Outline

Occasion and Continuity

We shall suppose that "Making Mercy a Way of Life" is the third in a series of eight studies on Christian virtues. The series is predominantly content-based, and it is the intent of the parish education board in charge of the adult education program to arrange for a number of followup sessions for general discussion purposes once the information base has been presented on the basis of the eight Scripture settings selected.

The initial session previewed the entire series, as well as exploring the first of the virtues, entitled Faithful Believers. This was followed by an investigation of perseverance entitled "Faithful unto the End." The present session will build upon faithfulness and perseverance, adding the quality of mercy in this continuing series of studies.

1. *Rozell's Complete Lessons*, vol. 31, Grand Rapids: Zondervan, 1977, pp. 60–65. ©by Lydia Rozell.

Goals

1. The Bible class will receive information about mercy, based on the Luke and 1 Corinthians readings. By means of lecture, outline, and added information available through media and overhead projector, members will strive for a basic understanding of the material.

2. Participants will be guided in applying the concepts to responsive living through a series of questions by the pastor. A major objective will be to understand that the Christian response to God's mercy is through a life of love in service to others.

Instructional Plan

Comment

I. Background Information and Introduction to Lesson and Lecture

President Lincoln was one of those rare men who could exemplify what Norman Cousins has called tenderness: "The highest expression of civilization is not art but the supreme tenderness that people who are strong enough, feel and show toward one another." This lesson provides a vivid contrast between callousness and mercy, between selfishness and extending oneself for the sake of others. Our age indeed needs to learn how to make mercy a way of life; Christians who have received God's mercy in Christ are to be at the head of the class when it comes to practical demonstrations of mercy.

The tie to Luke 13:10–17 is using the example of Christ Himself as a healer who, in mercy, showed patience and love in the midst of hatred and hypocrisy.

In setting up this session around the lecture, an introduction as it might be spoken is used to initiate thinking, pointing to the intent of the lesson's objectives.

The use of examples, just as in the case of parabolic illustrations, are only as good as the connection made. The point must be driven home by solid connection with the example given.

II. Lesson Sequence

A. Pre-session fellowship

B. Opening devotion, prayer (pastor)
Scripture Reading: Micah 7:18–20

Duration—5 minutes

C. The Lecture
Lecture Outline
1. Jesus' Mercy—his enemies' cruelty—Luke 13:10–17
  a) Jesus' healing of the infirm woman.
  b) Jesus is criticized by synagogue rulers and legalists.
  c) Jesus exposes the hypocrisy of the legalists.
  d) Summary: "Christ's answer (to the legalists) achieved something valuable: the hardhearted were put to shame while others were filled with joy. Jesus was not only superior intellectually; He won the people with His heart of tenderness. The Christian who would follow in the ways of Jesus must know the freedom of the gospel message and must practice its application."

A lecture outline awaits each member, to be picked up at coffee table.

Total time available for lecture represents one/third of Bible class hour.

The better lectures for instructional purposes take no chances with a direct move from section to section. Summaries en route are invaluable to audience understanding of the thrust and intent of the lecture.

2. Relinquishing freedom for the sake of others—I Corinthians 9:19–23

a) Paul explains his guiding principle to the Corinthians: He is free and yet a slave. Note Luther: "I am a slave to no man, but in all things, a servant to all." (v. 19).

Supportive references used at this point by means of overhead so that all may share. Galatians 2:11–21; Acts 18:18; 1 Corinthians 8:13 and Romans 14:21, all from overhead projection.

b) Paul applies the principle (vv. 20–22)
   (1) He was required to live like a Jew.
   (2) He was required to live like a Gentile.

c) The reason: this principle based on a desire expressed in verses 22–23. Tie in to Luke: putting top value on the gospel means to share in its blessings.

3. Concluding summary

"To be merciful is costly. It costs you yourself. It means self-denial and opening yourself to false allegations and criticism. The questions we have to decide are, Are the physical and spiritual needs of people worth it? and, Does the gospel itself demand it?"

The questions posed here will be used to initiate the discussion period.

Duration, C—20 minutes

Last question entertained at approximately 18 minutes.

III. Discussion

Leading questions prepared for discussion, to be used as circumstances suggest:

A. Two questions (above) from concluding summary

B. What approaches could members make to people that would be living testimony to the gospel? What are the risks involved in loving others; how does the risk put your Christianity on the line? (Personal experiences are welcome as examples, if members are so inclined.)

C. Concluding summary to discussion questions.

Duration, III—up to 20 minutes

IV. Summary and preview (pastor)

Summary developed on overhead transparency as discussion progresses.

A. Summary of salient issues as they become known through lecture and discussion. Members assist in summing up.

From prepared transparency, featuring suggested readings for session 4.

B. Preview, with short review of first and second session highlights. Emphasis: continuity.

Duration, IV—10 minutes

V. Closing devotion and prayer (elder)—

Duration—5 minutes

Time elapsed for session: ca. 60 minutes

A Final Observation

Before leaving these two studies, and with them the lecture-discussion method, a few final observations:

1. "Discipleship Demands Dedication" and "Making Mercy a

Way of Life," featuring as they do, two different approaches to this Bible class format, use a variety of speaking, listening, teaching, and participation skills. While moving through the different parts of the lessons' structure, a variety of activities beyond the lecture are at work. Nonetheless, the success of this setting is largely dependent on the skills brought to the class by the one who is very obviously in the driver's seat, the lecturer. That up-front person is going to have to be enthusiastic, entertaining, well prepared, and beyond all that, skilled at asking questions, sifting information, sensitive leadership. The lecturer must also be self-disciplined. Quite an order for anyone.

2. At first glance the two lecture-discussion outlines might appear to be labored and just too elaborate. Let me suggest that you give it a second or third try to get the feel and style of movement. I am certain you will find that most, and possibly all, of these outline parts have at one time or another been a part of your past Bible class experience. The outline, then, is a road map suggesting ways and means of getting from the goal, through the explanations and sequence, into the minds and active beings of the class members. But surely the bottom line in these considerations is that lecture-discussion as a method for use in Bible classes must be well organized, move crisply along, and involve the listeners meaningfully.

Forewarned is forearmed! Perhaps by looking the inherent weakness right in the eye and noting a few shortcomings, we can still use this time-honored strategy to the top of its potential, thereby doing both lecturers and listeners a great service in helping to equip the saints to be knowledgeable and strategically informed workers in Christ's kingdom!

Part

Equipping, Skills, and Mastery

What Skill Mastery Is All About

This strategy aims at analyzing, observing, practicing, and evaluating an activity, a series of actions, or a performance, for the purpose of mastering and performing a skill under varied conditions and circumstances.

Typical skill questions begin with words like: "How do I . . . ?" They provide an entree to instructional assistance that seeks either to introduce a particular capability or to develop it to even more sophisticated and artistic levels. The doing-acting-performing are what skill learning and skill mastery are all about.

Organizers and practitioners in adult Christian education have invested far too little time and effort in the crucial area of skill development for Kingdom building. Whatever the reasons, deliberate or unwitting, I fear we have suffered immeasurably as a consequence. Not only have we overlooked the basic nature of skill development, we have often deprived ourselves of a positive approach to adult involvement in learning, and ultimately of more capable, committed Christians.

Skill mastery is a bridge from presentation to exploration in adult Christian education. As such, it affords us opportunities not only to identify the many areas of need in skill development, but further and more importantly, it provides each of us with the challenge of developing our skills as we seek to build each other up in the faith and to extend our witness, under God, to an ever-widening circle of influence.

While there is so much more that can and should be done, we are not without a bright spot to serve as an example. That sunny ray has been provided by an outpouring of trained, purposeful activity during the seventies, known as the evangelism explosion. During that decade Christendom undertook a massive campaign of bringing the gospel to people on an unprecedented scale, involving Christians in training programs and evangelistic work that brought the Gospel to millions in the Americas alone.

No small part of that endeavor, which I can only pray will maintain its momentum, was the aspect of skill training that preceded this heartening, lay-oriented effort. Given the opportunity to learn about, practice, and hone their skills to a real evangelistic artistry under God's Spirit, His people, i.e., Christian adults, saw their efforts bountifully blessed.

The connection between the development of a skill, the involvement of the learner, the impetus to action and independent decision making—something adult educators hope for as the best of educational goals—must not escape our notice here. It should not be much of a trick to make the transfer to the many other areas of church life in need of attention, now should it?

This emphasis on skill mastery, then, serves several purposes:

1. to alert us to the need for the development and use of the many skills involved in Kingdom building;
2. to identify these many skills and begin teaching and learning them on an organized basis as an integral part of Kingdom building strategy;
3. to move into areas of adult education that address many of the concerns and needs people have both individually and corporately, and equip them to contribute meaningfully to the mission of the church in all its aspects of ministry; and
4. that the Scriptures be used as a primary source and inspiration for identification and training in skill learning so that both ability and power may stem from the source that alone can bless each effort.[1]

A Taxonomical Approach—Step by Step

Having given skill mastery a brief introductory overview, we turn at this point to analyzing its characteristics and instructional makeup. Our starting point in this regard is the recognition of its dual nature, borrowing as it does from the lecture and demonstration style, and employing such individualized means as one-to-one instruction, peer planning and evaluation,

1. It is, of course, God Himself who is the prime Kingdom builder. He does, however, accomplish the building of His temporal kingdom through His Word and, equally significant, through His people, by using those special skills we identify and in turn refine through searching His Word. We mention but three here: evangelism (2 Cor. 5:18–20), teaching (Acts 20:17–21), and prayer (1 Thess. 5:12–21).

and independent activity. These characteristics, and still others, are implicit in figure 3 and in the following explanation of the eight procedural steps.

Step 1: Skill Definition

In this step the learner or trainee is introduced to the skill. A lecturette which presents the background and related activities with which the skill is associated is an initial orientation point. The basics of skill performance, and its sequence of movement or operational steps are presented, often making use of illustrative aids such as film or stills.

Step 2: Skill Demonstration

The trainer demonstrates at appropriate speed each of the parts, or a combination of parts, that may comprise a unified whole. After repeating the demonstration of parts or sections, the trainer demonstrates the complete activity. It is important to note that, while it is not necessary that the leader be proficient at the skill, it *is* necessary that he or she know each step and be able, at least in a fundamental way, to demonstrate the skill under consideration.

Step 3: Statement of Performing Objective

Having seen the skill performed, the next step requires that a performing objective be given so that the trainees will know

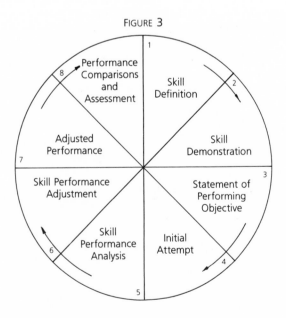

FIGURE 3

whether parts or the whole sequence of activities associated with the skill will be performed, and further, at what level of mastery. Before a start is made each participant should know and understand the requirements and expectations of the leader. The statement of the objective of skill performance is, therefore, very important because it sets a standard and clarifies the performer's perception of what must be done.

Step 4: Initial Attempt

This is the point at which the trainees begin to work toward the achievement of the performing objectives. Initial attempts are usually further divided into sections so that parts of the whole, if practicable, can be mastered under control. As proficiency increases each part is coordinated and unified into a single motion or activity until an appropriate performance speed and level are achieved. Initial attempts are made under peer and trainer observation.

Step 5: Skill Performance Analysis

Reviewing the performing objectives, the initial attempts at skill performance are analyzed and subsequently rated for further practice attempts, identifying those parts that have not been mastered. A review of basic information presented in step 1 might be advisable at this time. Trainees often perform poorly when understanding of the skill has not been grasped. Performance usually picks up when a review enables learners to associate the full range of activity with the skill training objective.

Step 6: Skill Performance Adjustment

At this point it should be possible to identify both strong and weak points in the trainee's performance. Appropriate adjustments can be made so that succeeding trials will move toward achieving the performance objectives. This step is achieved through analyzing what has been done *and* returning to the specific weakness or inability with the assistance of both trainers and peers.

Step 7: Adjusted Performance

Steps 5, 6, and 7 provide opportunity for the learner to do the skill. It is during step 7, however, that the repetition and practice, often in a solitary situation, begins to make a difference in performance. It is critically important that the learner not repeat mistakes as a part of the practice. Step 7 is a crossover step, linking 5 and 6 with 8. The ultimate success, as well as artistry with which the skill is performed, is dependent on both the expertise available for evaluation, and the willingness or determination of the trainee to master the skill. Adjusted performance is the key, practice is the prerequisite.

Step 8: Performance Comparisons and Assessment

Although this is not the final objective, it is a final part of the training, per se, inasmuch as comparisons with peer and professional performance provide indications with respect to mastery levels, and the distance remaining if personal, corporate, or performance standards in a given activity or field are to be achieved or even surpassed. At this stage gifted trainers or leaders are critically important. The greater their powers of observation and analysis, and their gifts of communication, the more likely performance will continue to improve. This step, finally, takes us back to step 1, where a review of definition may once again be in order, only from the vantage point of a still higher level of achievement. The cycle begins, then, all over.

There are a number of levels at which skills are performed. That was implicit in references to performance in steps 7 and 8. Four such levels are readily identifiable: (1) a novice level, (2) basic mastery, (3) advanced mastery, and (4) artistic performance level. An example of this sequence: (1) Novice: beginning piano; (2) basic mastery: performance at piano recital for a given level of skill (e.g., third grade solo level); (3) advanced mastery: international medal competition performance; and (4) artistic performance level: solo pianist for performing professional symphony orchestras. That same gradation can also be applied to skills or performance for various phases of church work.

These skill-mastery characteristics, outlined in sequence steps, seek to command our respectful attention. The reason? We have moved into the vitally important area of equipping God's people for ministry. That equipping is, to a great extent, a matter of training in skills. So it is well that we draw a bead on the many skills inherent in that ministry. And beyond that, this brief analysis of skills should suggest longer and more studied looks, on a continuing basis, of the needs of the church in this respect. That would, beyond a doubt, prompt a recognition of the fact that the work of the church is, to a great extent, skill oriented, and further, that such skills can, indeed must, be taught. Such a starter list, with an example for each entry, is shown in figure 4.

The task of skill development in the church can also be described in terms of the various ministries that comprise the mission of the church. The Scriptures outline six such ministries, each of which is empowered by God's Spirit and enacted

FIGURE 4   **Skill Categories: A Starter List**

Skill Category	Skill Type	Example
Mental Skills	Interpreting	Finding the meaning of a section of Scripture (the study of hermeneutics).
These skills feature the use of both calculative and intuitive capacities of the mind.	Analyzing	Reviewing the parables for the purpose of investigating teaching style.
	Researching	Studying the relationship of the Persian and Babylonian empires during the reign of Queen Esther.
	Systematizing	Arranging information about the doctrine of justification from the Book of Romans.
	Applying	Using an analysis of suffering on the basis of the Book of Job as background for a letter to a friend who is very ill.
	Reviewing	Collecting and collating material in three of Christ's miracles in digest form.
	Organizing	Arranging a presentation to the Bible class in outline form.
	Classifying	Identifying witnessing styles in the Book of Acts.
Other mental skills include:		Testing, distinguishing, diagnosing, calculating, dealing with spaces and shapes, composing, examining, sizing up a situation, imagining.
Adaptive Skills	Training	Preparing a group of people to interpret a section of the Scriptures.
These skills feature the capacity to shape, transform, adjust to, or remake the various environments and "climates" in which we live.	Negotiating	Coming to an agreement as to which of the major and minor prophets should be studied, and in which order.
	Following through	Participating in calls made on people who have been contacted about church membership, but who have not responded to the initial contact.
	Designing	Developing a format and scheme for an altar banner.
	Improvising	Using alternate approaches to illustrate a point when equipment breaks down.
	Coping	Managing circumstances under adverse conditions so that they may be made conducive to witnessing.
	Problem solving	This is the most complicated of all adaptive skills, a skill of maximum intellectual and adaptive demand. As part of the case-study strategy it will be analyzed and examined at that point.
Other adaptive skills include:		Inventing, regulating, experimenting, performing, learning how to learn, making decisions, adapting, fashioning, and sorting.
Interactive Skills	Helping	Working in a community relief program.
These skills feature interpersonal relationships and the conduct of human affairs.	Guiding	Helping the Scouts achieve merit badges.
	Teaching	Instructing the fourth-grade Sunday school class.

Showing sensitivity	Arranging and participating in Christmas caroling at the community hospital.
Serving as representative	Agreeing to represent the local congregation as delegate to the next plenary meeting of the denomination.
Caring	Reading to a blind member of the congregation.
Listening	Attentively listening to what people are saying and understanding their need through attending to their conversation.
Offering support	Volunteering to visit the sick and aged.
Other interactive skills include:	Counseling, concilliating, listening, enhancing relationships, persuading, compromising, empathizing, motivating, serving as mediator, healing, following, loving, and the numerous skills involved in family life, such as parenting.

on the basis of various skills: worship, proclamation, witnessing, teaching, service, and fellowship. Scripture references and examples of each appear in figure 5.

The many dimensions of skill development we have considered regarding its nature, scope, and characteristics, give us an indication of the immensity of the task confronting the church. And as if that were not enough, we are reminded by Paul that we are to use the Scriptures with diligence so that these skilled Christians may be thoroughly furnished, i.e., *equipped for every good work* (2 Tim. 3:16–17). Such an admonition challenges us to be about the entire range of God's business, and further, to do it to the very best of God-given ability. So we are here confronted with a man-sized—or more accurately put, God-sized—responsibility, one which only He, through His Word working in us, can begin to accomplish.

Strengths and Advantages

Skill-mastery has much to commend it as a strategy for the education of Christian adults. Skills that are useful in meeting the many responsibilities and situations encountered in daily living, as well as in crisis and problem areas, are high priority items among adults. There is no limit to the lengths they will go to master such skills. Relevance is, of course, the key. So long as a skill, or set of skills, is recognized and endorsed by the learners as helpful, they will strive to become proficient. That is an advantage that can also be turned toward ministry, thus providing blessings for the church while providing for the personal blessings of satisfaction and achievement.

The very nature of skill development involves each participant actively and personally. During the course of a skill

FIGURE 5   **Ministries Comprising the Mission
of the Church**

Ministry	Scripture	Examples
Worship	Col. 3:12–17	Praying Leading devotions Participating in the worship services

Proclamation	Luke 4:18	Proclaiming, i.e., telling the
		  Good News of reconciliation
		  of man with God through
		  Jesus Christ to people
		  everywhere
		Speaking the good word of the
		  gospel with winsome and
		  persuasive conviction

Witnessing	John 15:26–27	Confessing personal faith
		Defending God's truth
		Doing God's will through
		  purposeful living
		Testifying of Christ's love
		  and lordship in all
		  situations

Teaching	2 Tim. 3:16–17	Guiding learning Counseling Developing skills

Service	Acts 11:27–30	Caring for and managing all
		  of God's gifts
		Engaging in social services
		  under the impulse of
		  Christian charity
		Assisting families in need

Fellowship	Acts 2:41–47	Loving one another Sharing God's blessings Communing together in unity Bringing others into fellowship

development sequence there is repeated contact with peers and instructors. That makes it potentially a strategy that features supportive interpersonal relationships. On most counts, therefore, we find this strategy highly effective, one that meets the requirements of educational activity at the adult level.

Limitations

Learning and mastering a skill is simply not everyone's cup of tea. Not every adult perceives the value or usefulness of the skills being taught. For those who are reluctant or just too shy to attempt a new or seemingly difficult activity, it can be outright traumatic regardless its potential. Consequently, motivational problems may surface and can be restrictive factors in skill development.

Another inhibiting factor may be the complicated nature of

the skill. There must be a balance between challenge and achievability for each individual learner. Continued or unresolved frustration soon takes its toll, and that is usually registered in lack of interest and reluctance to keep on trying until each part is under control.

Teachers or trainers can also be limiting factors, particularly if they are highly proficient at the skill they are teaching. It often happens that highly successful or artistic people have little patience with "a fumbling beginner." Or, if instructors fail to break down the skill into its various components, the learners will struggle in their attempts to bring the various parts into a unified whole.

Finally, those being trained in a particular skill may actually be beyond the point of training at a given stage; or conversely, not up to a point where it is possible to integrate the component parts into a pattern. Put simply: we are not *all* at the same place at the same time. Perceptive instructors and patient learners can offset such a limitation, but variables such as time limitations and personal investment often militate against even those who are inclined to be more patient.

Participation Pointers

Skills are learned and refined by doing them. One has to try. The first and foremost participation pointer, therefore, is to meet the challenge head on. Having determined to get the skill under control, we can move on to a second point, that of recognizing the pattern of interlocking operations or activities which in sum make up the entire sequence. That is an analytical task that will no doubt call for assistance, However, it is the learner's responsibility to get the sequence and all the working parts under control for himself.

The psychological factor in adult skill development is immense. For example, until one has granted himself or herself the permission, as it were, to try, fail, and try again, all the coaching and reassurances of peers or instructors will have little effect on progression and ultimate mastery. Wishing simply will not make it so, and for many, being confronted with apparent intricacies or initially complex steps to follow, there is in such complexity an open invitation to retreat. But instructors are on the scene to assist the learners, so it pays for the participant to persevere, to keep coming back at instructors and peers, reminding them that their expertise and support are needed as all move toward the goal of mastery.

It is well to remember that the greater goal of putting the skill to use in the larger framework of ministry to people is a means to an end greater than either skill mastery or artistic performance. That should assist us in keeping trials, errors, artistry, or reluctance in proper perspective, enabling us to get over those inevitable rough spots.

All Things Considered

The mastery of skills, while demanding, is a source of great personal satisfaction and, further, prepares us for ever greater opportunities to serve. Thus, the teaching and learning aspect of skill mastery can be, within its proper parameters, a premier example of educational methodology at the adult level. I have rarely experienced a dull or unproductive skill training session. The requirements, principles, and standards for highly productive instructional activity designed for adults correlate so strongly with skill development that it is almost a sure-fire strategy every time out. What more could one hope for in our very complex social order, and in our active congregational programs, as well.

Skill-Mastery Unit I

That Is to Say

A four-session study in developing Biblical interpretation skills, featuring an investigation of forty-eight separate Scriptural references.

Unit Goals

1. The adult Bible class will strive to develop and master effective referencing skills through the use of the *Thompson Chain Reference Bible* system (figure 6).

2. Class members will learn about, develop, and begin to master at least three fundamental skills for use in Biblical interpretation: (a) the Scriptures interpret themselves, (b) clear passages in the Scriptures establish Christianity's cardinal teachings, and (c) the gospel and context establish perspective for passages of the Scriptures.

Session 1: Using Your Bible Skillfully

This is the initial session in a series of lessons designed to develop, master, and apply skills in Biblical interpretation. The unit's title, "That Is to Say . . . ," has as its primary purpose drawing our attention to the place and process of comparison, meaning, and application of principle to Biblical study. The four lessons look not only at interpretation, but as in the case of this initial lesson, they introduce members to Biblical study in general, with a special emphasis on reference work.

FIGURE 6 **Facsimile Page from *Thompson Chain Reference Bible***

① INTRODUCTION OF THE BOOK
These *four topics* form a suggestive Introduction to the Book. The Pilot Numbers at the *left* of the first two topics lead to a complete *analysis* of the *epistle* and also an *analysis* of the *author*.

② PILOT NUMBER
The "Pilot Number" in the numerical system—at the *left* of the topics on the margin—leads directly to the same *topic* in the Comprehensive Helps *section* where all references are found and desired information provided.

③ FORWARD REFERENCE IN CHAIN
The reference printed at the *right* of a topic is the "Forward Reference" which leads to the end of the 'chain.' One obtains each reference in its Scriptural setting by following a 'chain.'

④ BIOGRAPHICAL STUDIES
The Text Cyclopedia *section* provides facts regarding Bible characters together with *citation* of Bible references about each; all important *characters are analyzed* and their *main characteristics* listed. In addition, the Biographical Analysis *section* aids in complete study of outstanding Bible Characters. Bible heroes "walk across the stage of life" again to furnish lessons and inspiring examples for all believers.

⑤ ANALYSIS OF CHAPTER
Each Chapter of the New Testament has been *thoroughly analyzed* into the *main divisions* and printed in **bold-face** type. They present a complete digest of the teachings of the Chapter.

⑥ TOPICAL SUB-DIVISIONS
Numerals or *letters* in *parentheses* at the *right* of a topic refer to subdivisions of topics in the Comprehensive Helps section.

⑦ SELF-PRONOUNCING DICTIONARY
Bible Dictionary material is included in Text Cyclopedia section. Names appearing in the Text are self-pronouncing.

⑧ ANALYSIS OF VERSE
Every important verse of the Old and New Testaments has been *analyzed* into topics which help to open up the meaning of the verses and to stimulate Bible study.

⑨ MODERN SUBJECTS TREATED
Adapted to the pace of the 20th Century, it gives the Bible teaching on subjects of everyday interest, which makes study even more interesting. Many such subjects, not even mentioned in other Bibles, are fully treated.

⑩ SPIRITUAL SUBJECTS EMPHASIZED
More spiritual references than any other reference Bible.

⑪ UNIQUE THUMB INDEX
In addition to the regular *black index tabs*, the principal divisions of the Books of the Bible are shown by *gold index tabs*. A total of **33 Index Tabs** for quick study reference.

OTHER PAGE FEATURES NOT SHOWN

PARALLELED PASSAGES
The parallel passages are marked on the margin. These are minor references prepared by a thorough revision of the old reference systems.

UNUSUAL SELECTION OF REFERENCES
Note that these subjects are not mentioned in verse. All references in Comprehensive Helps under subjects are selected because of thought rather than word. This is a great advantage even over a complete Concordance.

THE EPISTLE OF PAUL TO
TITUS

CHAPTER 1

Why Titus was left in Crete. 6 How ministers should be qualified, etc.

PAUL, a servant of God, and an apostle of Jḗsus Christ, according to the faith of God's elect, and the acknowledging of the truth which is after godliness;

2 In hope of eternal life, which God, that cannot lie, promised before the world began;

3 But hath in due times manifested his word through preaching, which is committed unto me according to the commandment of God our Saviour;

4 To Titus, *mine* own son after the common faith: Grace, mercy, *and* peace, from God the Father and the Lord Jḗsus Christ our Saviour.

5 For this cause left I thee in Crēte, that thou shouldest set in order the things that are wanting, and ordain elders in every city, as I had appointed thee:

6 If any be blameless, the husband of one wife, having faithful children not accused of riot or unruly.

7 For a bishop must be blameless, as the steward of God; not selfwilled, not soon angry,

14 Not giving heed to Jewish fables, and commandments of men, that turn from the truth.

15 Unto the pure all things *are* pure: but unto them that are defiled and unbelieving *is* nothing pure; but even their mind and conscience is defiled.

16 They profess that they know God; but in works they deny *him*, being abominable, and disobedient, and unto every good work reprobate.

CHAPTER 2

Directions given to Titus. 11 *What the gospel teacheth.*

BUT speak thou the things which become sound doctrine:

2 That the aged men be sober, grave, temperate, sound in faith, in charity, in patience.

3 The aged women likewise, that *they be* in behaviour as becometh holiness, not false accusers, not given to much wine, teachers of good things;

4 That they may teach the young women to be sober, to love their husbands, to love their children,

5 *To be* discreet, chaste, keepers at home, good, obedient to their own husbands, that the word of God be not blasphemed.

6 Young men likewise exhort

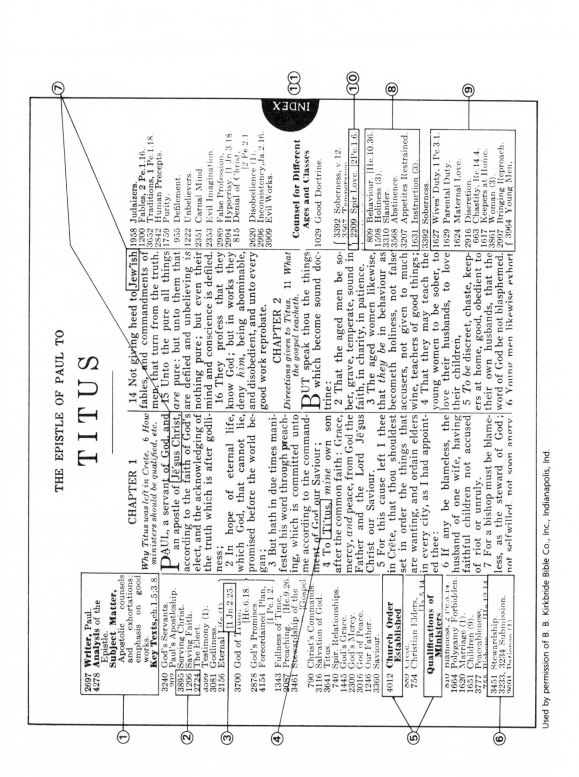

INDEX

Used by permission of B. B. Kirkbride Bible Co., Inc., Indianapolis, Ind.

Interpretation is a mental skill (figure 4, Skill Categories) and one that all members use again and again. It is especially useful in such ministries as witnessing and teaching, but also, from time to time, in service and in fellowship. The overall goal of these four lessons is to equip Bible class members to make effective as well as efficient use of their Bibles, and understand the Bible according to consistent principles of interpretation. In order to solidify the skill, ample opportunity is provided for practice. The overarching goal in this training for mastery is to enable the members to read, interpret, and apply the Bible independently and under varying conditions or situations.

Setting and Learners

Settings affect teaching and learning from the standpoint of their impact both tactically and psychologically. In fact the setting has a decisive impact on the achievement of educational goals. If the goal happens to involve scholarship the setting must aid and abet scholarly activity. Therefore, this series of sessions on Biblical interpretation should be conducted in an environment featuring educational facilities that enable the learners to get at the task efficiently and productively.

In order to accommodate the thirty-plus members anticipated, the site selected is a large, open room which, though spacious, is well-lit, comfortably furnished, and pleasing to the eye. Such a place often turns out to be the basement of the church itself or a wing of the church used for fellowship purposes or a room in an adjacent building. There is no reason that these rooms cannot be properly appointed for many purposes, but *care must be taken to actually create the appropriate setting.*

In the site selected for these sessions ten tables are distributed throughout the room, and six are set up for six members per table. Each study table is provided with *Thompson Chain Reference Bibles* and suffcent supplies of paper and outlines. Members are presented with suitable folders for use throughout the series. Four additional tables with displays of reference works and several Bibles of varying types are arranged around the study tables. The leader, in this case the pastor, is positioned at a smaller table furnished with an overhead projector and a table lectern. Behind him is a suspended screen for use during the session. The setting, therefore, not only aims at providing for an easy informality by using individualized groupings but also seeks to provide an adequate environment for concentrated, scholarly activity.

This detailed description of setting is presumed to be constant throughout the series; the setting and learner segment of the instructional plan will not, therefore, be repeated.

Lesson Theme

Lesson themes in this series will be taken from the title of the individual session. This lesson's theme is "Using Your Bible Skillfully."

Lesson Outline

Occasion and Continuity

This leadoff lesson seeks to set the pace, tone, and quality of the entire unit. Though short, the unit provides for mastering enough skills to enable the membership to achieve a basic mastery level in Biblical interpretation. The initial session, like each succeeding one, lasts approximately ninety minutes. It previews each of the skills and overall goals, as well as focuses on the approach and actual handling of the Bible as a primary basis for research and study.

Goals

1. In this session the adult Bible class members will be presented with an overview of the entire course, which highlights reference work in the Bible, and several basic principles of Biblical interpretation. They will use the outline material provided in their folders for additional notations to the major features presented.

2. The members will practice skill mastery according to the outline (cf. figure 3, Skill Mastery: A Taxonomical Approach) also provided in their folders.

3. Members will also strive to make substantial progress toward the achievement of one of the unit goals: making efficient and effective use of their Bibles. This will be accomplished by studying the layout of a reference Bible and by working with a *Thompson Chain Reference Bible* and with one other Bible of personal choice as several prototype samplings are tested.

Instructional Plan	Comment
I. Opening devotion based on 2 Peter 1:19: "We have also a more sure word of prophecy; whereunto ye do well that ye take heed, as unto a light that shineth in a dark place, until the day dawn, and the daystar arise in your hearts." *Duration*—5 minutes	
II. Orientation to *That Is to Say* . . . , preview of 4 sessions, and introduction to style, format (A brief review of Skill-Mastery: A Taxonomical Approach, so that members understand how sessions are arranged) *Duration*—15 minutes	The three goals for the evening's work are prominently displayed near the head table, and the goals for the unit are also

displayed. At each table folders are available containing the materials for use during the session.

III. Biblical referencing skills explained

  A. Examination of several Bible arrangements, noting especially central column reference listings

Folder displays include Thompson sample display and outline of presentation.

  B. Examination of Thompson sample display, figure 6

Use of overhead projector for emphasis and clarity.

Duration, III—10 minutes

IV. Skill demonstration following the display outline; members follow example based on Titus 1:14. Pilot Number 1200 used as example (connection with 2 Peter 1:19 devotion).
    Duration—10 minutes

Point to goals display; refer repeatedly to all goals.

V. Goals for the session reviewed: Special emphasis, B of lesson outline.
    Duration—5 minutes

BREAK

Examples for trials:
John 3:16
Matthew 16:15–16
Tables may work jointly or by couples in referencing.

VI. Initial attempts, emphasizing cross referencing before chains are attempted.

    Duration—10 minutes

By couples and by table so that there is solid peer support. Leader (pastor) visits each table.

VII. Performance analysis and performance adjustments

    Duration—10 minutes

Performing either individually or by couple, depending on personal preference.

VIII. Adjusted performance

Members may select one or more examples, but skill *mastery* should be emphasized, not speed or quantity.

    Trial examples: Psalm 119:162–63; Malachi 3:10; Ephesians 4:23–24

    Duration—15 minutes

If members are willing to take the time, one or two examples might be demonstrated by group members.

A few more examples might be given for trials between sessions.

IX. Preview and final assessment

    Duration—5 minutes

X. Closing devotion

Highlights ahead should accent continuing mastery and continuity.

    Duration—5 minutes

    Time elapsed for session: ca. 90 minutes

A Final Observation

The outline of this instructional session may appear to hang heavy with practice time. However, that time is well spent. There are reasons for our limited range of skills, especially in church work. In the first place, we need to develop a consciousness of the many skills, and what they enable us to do, and then, we have to go about the sometimes tedious business of learning them so that through a mastery of the capability, we may serve the church effectively. And in the midst of these concerns stands the overlooked element of time. Without deliberate management of the time-blocks we provide for teaching and learning, we often succumb to the temptation of lecturing the time away (as teachers), or letting Charlie do it (as lay people). No skill was ever mastered that way. So this initial session gets right on down to the critical business of getting people "at it," while simultaneously forcing the pastor-trainer to choose his words and demonstrations with utmost care for the limited time available. Thus, the pace is set for the succeeding sessions.

Session 2: Meanings, Scripture, and You

This lesson will actually emphasize skills of biblical interpretation. The work in this session is more demanding and successes will be harder won. Consequently, words to the wise concerning the stepped-up challenge are in order.

The lesson title spotlights three major issues concerning the Bible's message to mankind: (a) the central position of the Scriptures in context and their unique power as special revelation; (b) the meanings we attach to its words; and (c) the target of that message, viz., we, the readers. The instructional strategy will of necessity have to emphasize the skill of interpretation as basic to the mastery of the several items treated, lest the session lose its way under the influence of its interlocking parts as they each vie for attention. The goals and sequence, therefore, are tailored to a tight fit. Continuity, review, and preview are prime teaching, as well as learning concerns. They are vital in tying all the strands meaningfully together.

"Meanings, Scripture, and You" aims at getting across this pivotal principle of Biblical interpretation: The Bible is its *own* interpreter. That principle is central to all others. It, therefore, leads the way and provides a foundation piece for the remaining skills in the unit.

Lesson Theme

The lesson stresses the Bible's preeminent position in interpretation. "Meanings, Scripture, and You," points up the interlocking nature of the meaning of the scriptural message and mankind, for whom that saving message is intended.

Lesson Outline

Occasion and Continuity

This second, ninety-minute session is scheduled for one week after the series opener, a pattern often followed in adult Christian education. That will have its own implications for instructional strategy, as well as for skill mastery. Consequently, it is necessary to make strong connections between the emphasis on Biblical usage and the central role of the Scriptures in the skills of Biblical interpretation. Continuity can be established from the point of the opening devotion forward, featuring key link points with concepts, skills, and even unit or lesson names.

The introduction part of the instructional sequence might well emphasize a quick run-through of major features to expedite the carryover from the past week's work. A rerun of one or several of the overhead transparencies developed for the initial session might be especially helpful for this purpose. Such time is well spent, especially for those who were absent or for those who may not have had the time to review or practice skills developed the previous week.

For those who either missed the unit opener or are not able to be present for "Meanings, Scripture, and You," special arrangements, previously made as a part of the organization of the instructional plan, must be called into action. Participants and leaders alike can only hope that the membership will be able to be present for each of the sessions. Contingency planning only goes so far, as well we know, before limited levels of achievement actually become counterproductive.

Goals

1. Guided by the pastor, Bible class members will review basic Biblical usage skills and preview the first of the interpretation skills: the Bible is its own interpreter.

2. The participants as a unit will begin to understand that mankind's reconciliation with God through Jesus Christ is the central meaning of the Bible's message, and apply it to the interpretation of several sample passages.

3. Working in units of six each (table partners) members will investigate 2 Peter 1:20–21, building on their work in lesson 1, to understand the basis for the Scripture-interprets-Scripture principle, as they trace parallel passages and other supportive evidence in cross-referencing.

4. Bible class members will work in couples with selected references to achieve a basic mastery of the Scripture-interprets-Scripture principle.

Instructional Plan

Comment

I. Opening devotion based on 2 Peter 1:12–21, with special emphasis on verses 19–21

Duration—5 minutes

Review and preview, the challenges ahead, and linking references to 2 Peter passage used for opening in the unit's first lesson.

II. Statement of goals for *Meanings, Scripture, and You*

Handouts for folders and work during this session available at study tables. Goals displayed near head table.

III. Lecture-demonstration: Scripture-interprets-Scripture, each instructional goal reviewed as demonstration proceeds

A. initial emphasis: goal 2; Salvation and Biblical meaning

B. Members follow as pastor lectures and demonstrates from Psalm 27:1 (Old Testament), and Romans 5:6–11 (New Testament), with supportive referencing

Duration, II–III—25 minutes

Steps 1 and 2 of the mastery taxonomy are combined in this section.

Prepared transparencies for overhead projection will be helpful in presentation with parallel use of blackboard.

IV. Clarification of task, arrangements, and review of goals 3 and 4

Duration—5 minutes

BREAK

Making certain that members understand the what, why, and how of their task after the break.

V. Initial attempts and performance adjustments, beginning with 2 Peter 1:20–21, adding the following as time permits: Psalm 91:11–12 with Deuteronomy 6:16 (example for all tables); John 2:19; Matthew 18:19; 1 Corinthians 3:16; Isaiah 48:9; Joshua 7:11–12; Ephesians 2:8; John 8:58; and Genesis 2:17

Duration—25 minutes

Goal 3 is the prime target in this step. Peer support is essential, as is the pastor's visit to each table.

VI. Adjusted performance

A. Interpretation according to the Scripture-interprets-Scripture principle emphasizes context, personal meaning, and the comparison of one Scriptural section with another, as the work is done in couples, three per table

Various emphases and noteworthy pointers or reminders may be posted, as well as projected either by slide or by overhead projector.

B. At least three or four of the following passages should be referenced, with appropriate conclusions listed. The passages: Genesis 12 and Galatians 3; an intratestamental reference; Matthew 26:6 and Mark 14:3; Revelation 5:8; 1 Corinthians 10:31; and Exodus 19:3–6.

Duration, VI—15–20 minutes

Key teaching point for Biblical interpretation: Remind that the Holy Spirit is the true and actual interpreter of Scripture when the Scripture-interprets-Scripture principle is followed.

Tables cross-checking may assist in mastering the skill.

Review of major issues and combination of first and second lesson skills.

VII. Final review and assessment
        Preview of next lesson, building on first two sessions

    Duration—5–10 minutes

VIII. Closing devotion

    Duration—5 minutes

    Time elapsed for session: ca. 90 minutes

A Final Observation

With the conclusion of this lesson Bible class members have reached the halfway point in their abbreviated, yet basic course of study in Biblical interpretation. By this time they have been exposed to some twenty-five separate passages from the Bible that feature a variety of topics and interpretational challenges. There should be a fundamental command, along with building confidence in the group as a whole by this time. Those who are experiencing problems with concepts or procedure will have made themselves known to perceptive teachers. These are the people who will need patient assistance, perhaps some remedial work, and even an extra session should time permit. Lingering difficulties complicate the instructional task, and it should be evident that the final two sessions will be unproductive if all are not in a position of relative equality at the start of the third session.

Session 3: Interpretation and Faith

The words in the unit title, "That Is to Say . . . ," imply that an interpretation is about to follow something that has been written or spoken. Clarifying and understanding meanings undergird intelligent communication, and that, of course, points up the crucial nature of the task of interpretation. After an introductory lesson on Biblical usage skills, the first and foremost of the interpretation skills emphasized the preeminent position of the Bible itself in the interpretation of its message.

The next step follows as another important consideration. This step is outlined, studied, and developed as a skill under the lesson title, "Interpretation and Faith," which stresses the relationship between interpretation and the faith of the believer. Consequently, the lesson aims at understandings as well as skill development. This, and other instructional considerations will need careful attention. For example, the pivotal position of this lesson in the unit of four suggests that the work be arranged so that members may review, with a conscious determination to set the steps in progressive order, what has preceded the present lesson. Then the task of further developing the skill itself may be continued.

A lesson of this type offers an opportunity to point out a very fundamental consideration in the teaching and learning situation. At the base of skill teaching is knowledge and understanding, the two most fundamental aspects of cognitive structure. That is why the very first step outlined in "Skill Mastery: A Taxonomical Approach" (figure 3) is one in which the definition of the skill takes the instructional form of a presentation, the methodology that commonly employs lecture, film, or demonstrations as its strategy for instruction.

Lesson Theme

This lesson's theme is "Interpretation and Faith." It not only adds to the progression of steps in mastering the skills of Biblical interpretation, but seeks also to emphasize the power of God's Word as a source of assured comfort and confidence to the membership through the clarity of the cardinal teachings its words contain.

Lesson Outline

Occasion and Continuity

By the time adult Bible class members have gathered for their third session in this unit they will have logged some three or four hours together, achieved a number of instructional (as well as personal) goals, and developed some momentum toward mastering the unit goals. This session offers a different kind of challenge in that its goals are not exclusively skill-oriented. This time there will be a pointed effort to capitalize on building an esprit de corps, aiming at attitudinal goals, as well as further skill mastery.

The point should be made that *skill development is not merely or exclusively a matter of mastering technique*. The vitally important psychological dimensions of attitude figure significantly in the entire process. This is especially true in the use of the Scriptures.

For the sake of drawing these interrelated instructional and devotional factors together, an expanded, ten-minute opening devotion, used to keynote as well as harmonize the elements of the three sessions, is suggested. A further aid to continuity would be the posting of instructional goals for the first two sessions on either side of the goals for "Interpretation and Faith."

Goals

1. Bible class members will review cross reference skills and the Scripture-interprets-Scripture principle by completing one of a number of optional exercises.

2. Members will strive to master the principle that the clear passages of Scripture establish cardinal Scriptural teachings, applying it as an interpretation skill.

3. The membership will seek to relate interpretation skills to the building of faith through the formulation of one cardinal teaching on the basis of interpretation principles, applying the skill under direction of the Holy Spirit through the use of the Scriptures.

Comment	Instructional Plan
Expanded time slot to include devotional accent on review, as well as preparation for session's work.	I. Opening devotion based on Romans 12:3–8. Accent keynotes an inspirational approach. *Duration*—10 minutes
Goals posted in a prominent position, session 3 goals posted higher than 1 and 2 on either side.	II. Reference to goals of first two sessions, statement of goals for "Interpretation and Faith"
Presentation outline available at coffee table for members' folders. Other materials for use available, at table, and color coded.	III. Pastoral presentation: A. Scriptures teach each cardinal article of faith clearly.
Overhead projection assists.	B. There is sufficient reinforcement to verify the cardinal teachings.
Greek: *analogia*, meaning "to compare"; comparison in Scripture for verification of cardinal teachings.	Demonstration, *a* and *b*, based on Matthew 5:45 (God cares for us) and related references.
A technical term: The Analogy of Faith, explanation, and comparison with Greek *analogia*.	Skill mastery techniques and interpretation review *Duration*, II–III—25 minutes
Special reference: Goals 1 and 2	IV. The task in perspective: review and clarification of goals for membership *Duration*—5 minutes
	BREAK
Initial attempt by tables, using 2 Timothy 3:14–15. The Scriptures assure us in the faith. Succeeding examples personally or in pairs.	V. Initial attempts and performance adjustments. Options: two or three from listing and one passage of personal preference. *Listing*: 1 John 3:9; 1 Corinthians 2:11–13; Luke 11:11–13; 1 Corinthians 5:19; and Joel 2:32

VI. Selection of one cardinal teaching from overhead projector listing for development, using two basic principles and *Thompson Chain Reference Bible*

Listing of options, with starter passages. Focus is on goal 3.

Duration, V–VI—25 minutes

Instructional assistance by pastor and appointed leaders.

VII. Adjusted performance
Review of the two basic interpretation principles with corrections for 5-b, followed by continued practice on one additional selection of a cardinal teaching from listing

Refer to 5-b and goal 3.

Duration—15 minutes

Total time for practice, including time spent under direction is ca. 65 minutes.

VIII. Review and preview
A view toward the last session based on accomplishments of sessions 1 through 3

A final recap of all major points summarized through overhead transparencies.

Duration—8 minutes

IX. Closing prayer

Duration—2 minutes

Time elapsed for session: ca, 90 minutes

A Final Observation

The basic foundation pieces of Biblical interpretation are now in place and have been practiced at some length. The two principles have also required continuing practice and improvement of the Biblical usage skills developed in the opening session. Inasmuch as the final session will add still another fast-paced study, involving context, human language and its part in the scheme of interpretation, and finally, the pivot point of interpretation, which is the gospel, it will be necesary to forge ahead without in-class attention to those who are a bit behind the pace set by the majority of Bible class members. Again, the caring spirit that pervades the group is the catalyst for individual assistance when and where needed between sessions. Both leaders and learners are responsible. Corporate success is limited where such a spirit is not pervasive as a positive factor in adult Christian education.

Session 4: Context, the Gospel, and Biblical Interpretation

The final session or final unit of study often prompts unrealistic expectations and their accompanying frustrations. Instructors as well as participants realize that not everything is going to turn out quite as well as might have been expected, and that in a few instances some of the goals will probably not be achieved at all. Under the crush of dwindling time there is, therefore, a strong temptation to make inordinate demands of the situation, the learners, and the instructor. That is usually spelled out in terms of attempting too much in an effort to squeeze in as much as possible before the final curtain rings down. On all counts this is a very bad risk and usually results in multiple losses. Not only do we forfeit time for review and evaluation that would solidify our gains; but further, we inevitably fare poorly with last minute pressures, or with a multiplicity of new ideas or skills, each of which clamors individually for the sustained attention we cannot give them. Consequently, we want to avoid these last minute disasters, planning our windup session in keeping with the style and pace all have come to expect, and making certain that the final topics and skills can be mastered with enough time reserved for a worthy review of the unit's work.

Accordingly, the approach to "Context, the Gospel, and Biblical Interpretation" emphasizes two areas of activity: the practice and mastery of the remaining skills and a review exercise that challenges the membership's mastery level as they employ each of the skills developed during the course of the unit.

Although not identified as such, we leave the "final exam," or the evaluation of progress during the course of the unit's work in the hands of this final review exercise. It will tell us all we need to know.

Lesson Theme

"Context, the Gospel, and Biblical Interpretation" addresses the final skill undertaken in this unit. Although that skill receives a prominent position in the sequence, the lesson also includes the use of that skill, along with others from previous sessions, in an interpretation exercise that calls on the integrative and organizational skills of the members. Context and the gospel message feature prominently in that exercise, thus underscoring the theme itself.

Lesson Outline

Occasion and Continuity

"That Is to Say . . . ," the title of our unit study, should have deepened significance as this final session unfolds. This is, as it were, the acid test, challenging our skills to bring forth valid meanings from the texts set before us. Therefore, the test of leadership also figures prominently, as we seek to weld together each of the former sessions, along with this final lesson, into a useful tool. A premium should be placed on quickened, though not distracting, pace, and each of the various parts of the sequence should move along decisively toward a final climax.

Goals

1. The membership will develop and begin to master the skill of using context properly in Biblical interpretation, viewing this and all other skills from the perspective of the gospel.

2. Members will interpret three texts as a review exercise in the mastery of interpretation skills.

3. The membership, with the pastor as leader, will review its work with a group critique of the skills and texts used in the review exercise.

Instructional Plan	Comment
I. Open with a devotional prayer based on Isaiah 34:16	
Duration—5 minutes	
II. The skill mastery sequence: Developing contextual skills, Using the gospel pivot point	The skill mastery sequence is altered to enable a group following of the lecture-demonstration, with use of overhead projections to illustrate each point. Participants work from materials provided for folders.
A. Combined presentation-demonstration on the basis of James 2:24–25 and Galatians 2:16, illustrating the contextual setting as interpretation guideline	
B. Adjustments, questions, and comments before completing cycle of mastery	
	Goal 1 is class objective.
C. Final practice and evaluation using an out-of-context passage: Matthew 6:16–18, with potential for interpretation error explained (Phil. 2:12 alternate)	*Note*: Scriptural interpretation from viewpoint of saving grace is stressed to bring perspective to message of Testament, book, greater context, and immediate passage structure.
Duration, II—15 minutes	
III. Bible class review of interpretation skills (sessions 1–4), using one setting from each Testament	Goal 2 is class objective.
One complete cycle, beginning with step 4 of Skill Mastery Taxonomy (figure 3), using:	Work may be done table by table, or one setting by tables and one setting as a class.
A. Old Testament, Isaiah 61:1–3;	Skills for Review: 1. Cross-referencing
B. New Testament, Mark 13:24–27. One or both passages may be used depending on time, but one should be completed	2. Scripture interprets itself 3. Clear passages provide basis for cardinal teachings.
Duration, III—15 minutes	4. Interpret on the
BREAK	basis of context, not

taking passages out
of context.
5. Gospel is pivot
point of interpreta-
tion.

Table groupings rea-
lign for different
viewpoints and com-
parisons.

IV. Review exercise in interpretation
Three scriptural contexts for the six tables, tables volunteering to take
contexts, two tables for each context. Skill mastery cycles begin with
step 4, objective already established as achievement of lesson goals 2
and 3.
Contexts include:

Table groups should
be alerted to follow-
up reporting on con-
texts as groups
evaluate skill mas-
tery and interpreta-
tions.

A. Romans 8:29 and 1 Peter 1:2. Comparison points from verb usage in
Acts 26:5; Romans 8:29; Acts 2:23; and 1 Peter 1:20
(*foreordained*).
Cardinal teaching: election, or predestination

B. Ephesians 2:4–9
Cardinal teaching: Our salvation depends on God's free and universal
grace alone.

Leaders and pastor
circulate freely to
participate and lead,
as well as counsel, as
groups work.

C. Acts 17:22–26
Cardinal teaching: It is God who upholds, governs, and directs
the world He created.

Duration, IV—20 minutes

Outline steps 5 and 6
aim at achieving goal
3.

V. Comparisons

Couples at tables compare their separate interpretations, sharing
information.

Duration—10 minutes

VI. Open discussion

Review *unit goals*.

Final summary review of skills and interpretations, each table
reporting and participating in large group discussion.

Duration—20 minutes

VII. Closing devotional prayer

Duration—5 minutes
Time elapsed for session: ca. 90 minutes

A Final Observation

"That Is to Say . . . ," concludes with the addition of a final
interpretation skill before beginning the all important work
of reviewing, summarizing, and solidifying the skills featured
in the four sessions. It must be admitted that these skills
are, indeed, quite fundamental, and that much more remains
to be done before one could actually lay claim to having mastered the skill, intricacies, and the art of Biblical interpretation. Yet, a beginning has been made, providing opportunity
to further these skills on the basis of a strong, reliable foundation.

A review of the lessons will reveal that rather large blocks of time are given to outright practice. That is exactly the way it should be if the ultimate aim is to *master* a skill, rather than talk about it. And that is what the goals of the unit, as well as each lesson, were all about!

10

Skill-Mastery Unit II

Listen—Hear!

A two-lesson unit on listening skills taken from a course on family-life skill development.

Unit Goals

The primary goal of session 1 is to develop understanding and insight, based on the Bible and skill-mastery practice, regarding the skills and role of listening in family-life relationships.

The primary goal of session 2 is to develop skills and appreciation with respect to attending, perceiving, caring, and active listening as a vital part of interpersonal and family-life relationships.

An Introductory Statement

The two skill-mastery lessons which comprise this short unit might very well occupy an up-front position in a course about family-life skills, parenting, or other similar types which accent the how-to's in skill development. The two lessons are designed as complimentary pieces, intended to form a solid, albeit brief, study of a single skill.

Because listening skills are so vitally important, and further, because the skill itself is essential to others in family-life concerns, the unit itself might well lead off an entire series, combining with as many as four to six major skills essential to

89

the Christian family setting. As many as ten to fourteen sessions might comprise the total course offering. This opening, two-lesson unit would be vital, therefore, from a number of instructional, as well as psychological, considerations.

The unit title, "Listen—Hear!" is an obvious play on words (and spelling!) intended to attract attention to the practice and art of listening, which involves us not only in a skill but in attitudes and outlook. Something so ostensibly easy, as least for those who *can* hear, is often carelessly, even thoughtlessly done. That can be maddening to those around us, especially in the family. All the more reason to prepare carefully and work diligently as the unit unfolds in the two longer evening sessions presented in this unit.

Recall, please, that listening skills are a part of that skill category which features interpersonal relationships and the conduct of human affairs. As such, it is an interactive skill and is included here because of its importance both in adult Christian education and in the lives of Christian family members everywhere.

Session 1: You Didn't Even Listen

The leadoff lesson in any course of study is in a most strategic position. It is placed in such prominence for some obvious reasons, one of which is, quite simply, that repeated use will no doubt be made of the information or skill developed. It is, therefore, considered fundamental to the remainder of the course work. There are other and equally compelling reasons to place a given lesson in the front position, but in the case of listening skills and their relationship to family life, we have an example of a fundamental skill that is essential to each succeeding session. It sets a pace and style and establishes a skill base to be called on again and again throughout the total number of sessions arranged.

The first of these tandem lessons in our unit, "Listen—Hear!" is designed as a two hour session. It will serve a number of purposes: as an orientation to family-life skills course work; to provide a rationale for the various sessions and the overall procedure; and to get down to the work scheduled for the unit. This initial session has its own provocative style and special flavor, and includes an instrumentation exercise to highlight the feel and accent of both lesson title and its intended emphases.

The session is developed with the basic skill mastery lines in mind, employing an instrumentation exercise as a part of step 4. Adjustments, appropriate instruction, and pointed references to the learning goals will be necessary in order to maintain perspective and to make constructive use of the sequenced activities.

Setting and Learners

A centrally located educational facility, part of a local congregation's church property, has been chosen as the site of a
twelve-session series entitled "Family-Life Skills Workshop." A
number of churches have combined to present this workshop for
their parish members. Approximately a hundred people have
responded, representing a wide range of ages. Teens, as well as
adults, have been invited to participate in family units. There is
a significant number of single participants. Coordination of
teaching personnel, scheduling, publicity, and materials has
been arranged by a central committee. Teachers and aides have
been trained in sufficient numbers to facilitate a varied instructional program. Large and small group work segments are
scheduled for each session. Each of the smaller groups will be
involved in the same activities so that all may benefit from the
same instruction and training in the various skills under consideration.

Sufficient time is alloted for a corporate opening devotional
worship, occasional group instructional demonstrations, and a
period of time each session for the comparison of small group
problems, issues, or questions. The total time given this evening's session is in the neighborhood of two hours, ninety
minutes of which is scheduled for small group instruction, using
the instructional plan.

Equipment and study materials are provided for the participants, and each room is prepared in advance for the special
purposes of the small groups. Provision for plenary sessions has
also been made. The host church has provided appropriate
folders and other materials as a starter-kit for each participant.

Lesson Theme

Three themes share equally important billing in this short
unit. While working under the individual session theme in the
first session, participants will want also to keep "Listen—
Hear!" the unit title in mind. These theme titles are meant to
attract attention, and they will call to mind the communication
problems most families face. The title of the first session, "You
Didn't Even Listen!" leads off with precisely that intention.

Lesson Outline

Occasion and Continuity

"You Didn't Even Listen!" gets this two-lesson unit off to a
fast start with a most suggestive title and, within its structure, a
sequence of activities designed to open people up, cause them to
think critically (but not negatively) about family communication problems, and to focus in particular on the art of listening.

As the lead lesson in a whole series of family-life skills, this one should provide occasion to develop not only a number of skills, but also to accent a positive attitudinal framework as high priority goals. Such an accomplishment would surely set a constructive and supportive pace for the course work ahead. That is a basic necessity in any case, but is especially noteworthy in a situation in which a wide age range and family interactions may tend to complicate the situation psychologically. Consequently, a word to wise leaders and participants: in such circumstances, care and concern, perceptive leadership, and compassionate participants are sine qua non to successful, edifying achievements.

Goals

1. Participants will begin to develop skills in listening, starting with the essential features of respect for personhood and attending.

2. Family-Life Skills Workshop attendants will participate in *Leveling: Giving and Receiving Adverse Feedback*, an exercise designed to consider, analyze, and legitimize negative responses in the communication process.

3. Participants will begin to appreciate the role of listening in interpersonal relationships.

4. Those attending will examine and begin to understand what the Bible says about interpersonal relationships and communication processes in family-life settings.

Comment

Instructional Plan

I. Workshop Opening:
Invocational hymn, reading (John 5:19–29), brief sermonette on the reading, and prayer.

Note: Prior arrangements have been made for teaching assignments for each group; each group works with the same basic instructional plan and reconvenes in plenary session as the last scheduled activity of the evening.

II. Welcome and orientation:

A. announcements about facilities, materials, workshop folders, and registration.

B. assignment of leaders, color-coded participation groupings, and rooms for group work.

Duration, I–II—up to 15 minutes

III. In each room a display of instructional objectives for the workshop session is posted. The instructional plan, along with statement of objectives is also provided in each folder, along with instructional materials and necessary handouts.
Instruction actually begins with a restatement of goals.

IV. You Didn't Even Listen, Pharaoh!

A. Exodus, chapters 5–11; final and special emphasis on Exodus 11:9.

B. Leader guides discussion on deaf ears and family problems. Additional Scripture settings include: Ephesians 1:7–14; Daniel 9:1–19 (especially vv. 17–19); and John 6:52–65.

C. One family problem: Luke 15:11–32, and the many perceptions of listening and hearing in the Luke account.

Duration, III–IV—up to 35 minutes

BREAK

V. Instrumentation Exercise:
Leveling: Giving and Receiving Adverse Feedback[1]

A. Goals

1. To let participants compare their perceptions of how a group sees them with the actual feedback obtained from the group.
2. To legitimize giving negative feedback within a group.
3. To develop skills in giving negative feedback.

B. Group Size
Eight to twelve participants

C. Time Required
Approximately ten minutes per participant.

D. Materials
Paper and pencil for each participant.

E. Physical Setting

1. Participants are seated in a circle for the first phase.
2. Participants are seated in a semicircle, with one chair "on stage" facing the semicircle, for the second phase (see figure 7).

F. Process

1. The facilitator discusses the goals of the exercise.
2. Paper and pencils are distributed, and participants are instructed to write down the first names of all group members. This list should begin with the facilitator and proceed clockwise. Names should be written down the left-hand side of the paper, with a space between each name.
3. Individuals are instructed to write a short piece of adverse feedback about each participant, including the facilitator and himself. The facilitator points out the following:
   a) Feedback will be given anonymously.
   b) The feedback should consist of a list of three to five adjectives rather than a sentence.
   c) Each participant *must* comment on every other participant.
   d) This task should take about fifteen minutes.
4. The papers are collected by the facilitator.
5. For the second phase of the exercise, chairs are rearranged according to the diagram in *Physical Setting*.
6. If there are no volunteers to be the first to receive feedback, the facilitator designates one member.
7. The format for this phase is divided into four parts.

Emphasis to this point: Goals 3 and 4.

Note: This exercise will be conducted as outlined in folder materials, with one exception; each participant is in the feedback receiving position for five, instead of the indicated ten minutes. Agenda item 8, leveling outline, calls for a summary discussion. This discussion should emphasize listening and interpersonal relationships.

Instrumentation exercise aims at goals 1 and 2. This segment of the instructional outline should be confined to fifty minutes if at all possible.

Note: Discussions, feedback, and interactions should feature insights developed during the scriptural study segment.

1. From *A Handbook of Structured Experiences for Human Relations Training*, Volume 1, revised, J. William Pfeiffer and John E. Jones, editors. Copyright 1969, 1974 by University Associates Publishers, Inc., San Diego, Calif. Used by permission.

FIGURE 7 **Seating Arrangement for Leveling**

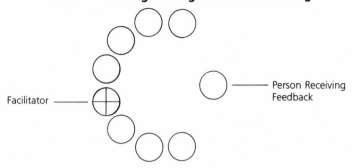

Part one consists of each individual anticipating adverse feedback he expects to receive and telling the group about it briefly.

Part two consists of reading the comments about an individual.

Part three consists of the individual comparing the degree of agreement between anticipated perception and actual perception.

Part four consists of exploring the individual's feeling reactions to adverse feedback. (The group in the semicircle should be asked not to react, either verbally or nonverbally, to the person receiving feedback at this time, to prevent an overload of feedback.) Each person who has received feedback chooses his successor to go "on stage," and the process is repeated.

8. The facilitator leads a discussion about the exercise, focusing on the stated goals.

G. Variations

1. Content of feedback could be changed to include positive data.

2. Feedback can be given face-to-face rather than anonymously.

3. The feedback sheet could be cut into strips and distributed by participants to each other. Strips may be taped onto a sheet of newsprint to make a poster for each participant. (One poster is made at a time.)

4. The individual being focused on may leave the room while the rest attempt to reach consensus about his adverse feedback. (This heightens the possibility that feedback will be honest and straightforward.)

Duration—up to 50 minutes

VI. Family-Life Skills Workshop Reconvening:

A. Leaders report on shared findings and insights to plenary session.

B. Open discussion on skills, problems, and approaches.

Duration—up to 20 minutes

VII. Closing hymn, devotion, and prayer.

Time elapsed for session: ca. 2 hours.

A Final Observation

You will undoubtedly have noticed that the skill mastery sequence outlined for previous lessons was not used in the instructional plan for "You Didn't Even Listen!" Each of the sequence steps can, however, be easily accounted for in the various segments of the session. If the intent is to concentrate exclusively on each skill involved, then there simply will not be enough time to accomplish all. During the evening's session steps 1–4 are to receive heavy emphasis. Those skills incidentally learned, such as those in the instrumentation exercise, will have to be encountered and mastered as the session progresses. Time is on the side of the instructor at least in this respect: steps 5–8 will receive adequate attention as the course progresses.

Session 2: You Heard Me Right!

This brief unit concludes with a lesson that is complimentary to, and builds on, the initial lesson of the previous week. Its time frame has been expanded by thirty minutes in order to accommodate a number of learning activities and continued skill practice. "You Heard Me Right!" offers another opportunity to participate in an instrumentation exercise to help achieve skill mastery goals, and further, to complete the lead-off series in this course which emphasizes a number of family-life and interpersonal relationship skills. A number of assumptions are made as this session commences; the participants have had an evening's experience behind them, enabling them to respond to the various settings and instructional activities with greater ease and efficiency; and they begin to see how family life and group interactions depend on listening skills.

While the title of the first lesson, worded as a somewhat negative warning, emphasized the hazards of careless or inattentive listening, thus jeopardizing communication as well as interpersonal relationships, this second part of the unit sets about the very constructive task of mastering skills that are a part of keen attention, interest in others, and an edifying spirit. "You Heard Me Right!" tried to capture that spirit by emphasizing attending skills. Such skills are implicit in the lesson's title. The contrast between the two lessons, thus, will not escape notice.

Setting and Learners

The style and format of this series will be reemphasized by a repeat of the previous week's schedule, as well as a repetition of some of the instructional activities. Instructional personnel will be requested to provide statements linking last week's work and this lesson, and further, with the Family-Life Skills Workshop goals. We might also assume that some of the kinks have been worked out of the schedule and procedure so that this second evening will move along in a more informed, forthright manner for both leaders and participants. Then too, the intervening week will have given each participant additional time to think about some of the Scriptural principles studied, and an opportunity now and then to practice the skills that emphasized respect for personhood, attention, and communicating within the context of family life.

Lesson Theme

The theme for this evening's work emphasizes the relationship between active, attentive listening and the building of God-pleasing interpersonal relationships. The focus is again on the family unit, but is not restricted exclusively to that setting. "You Heard Me Right!" is a title that suggests attentive listening has been going on, providing a basis for the kind of supportive, caring relationships that can develop in the Christian family, as well as in dealings with others. While this theme might look, quite restrictive at first glance, it should develop a broader emphasis as the session progresses, thus enabling the participants to grasp a wider scope of meaning as they move from the conclusion of this lesson to other skills the workshop will feature in the weeks to come.

Lesson Outline

Occasion and Continuity

Ample indication of both the occasion for the session and the continuity developed to this point have been given. However, it is well to note that in a short unit of only two lessons, we are well advised to stress the position of the unit, as well as its individual lessons, in the overall scheme of things. Therefore, pointed references to unit names, individual session emphases, and workshop goals are in order. Ultimately, that will produce a cohesive, well-ordered whole.

Goals

1. The workshop participants will add to the skills of attending and active listening, those involving perceptivity and responsive interactions in communications within family-life settings.

2. Participants will consult the Scriptures as they continue to seek insight concerning relationship building based on an understanding of the Bible's message regarding family-life relationships.

3. Participants will be involved in an instrumentation exer-

cise designed to link behaviors to perceptions, establish an appropriate climate for family-life communication, and to continue practicing active listening skills.

Note: These goals represent step 3 of the skill mastery sequence in figure 3 and should be prominently displayed as skill mastery objectives for each skill reviewed and practiced.

Instructional Plan

I. Opening hymn and prayer (plenary session opening) Scripture reading: Psalm 84

II. Orientation, instructions for participants, groups, and instructors. Worksheets and handouts available at individual rooms. Agendas and further explanations available for workshop folders at assigned rooms.

Duration, I–II—up to 10 minutes

III. Instrumentation exercise at assigned rooms.
   I Hear That You . . .[1]

   A. Goals for this exercise
      1. To establish a climate conducive to giving and receiving responses in family life and interpersonal relationships in working group settings
      2. To practice active listening and responding skills
      3. To help make family members' behavior more understandable by linking their behavior patterns to perceptions
      4. To assist in improving family life and interpersonal relationships

   B. Setting, time, materials
      Group size should include no more than ten members. Participants will need blank paper, pencils, newsprint, and a felt-tipped marker. Provide a room large enough to accommodate pairings from within the small group designations who cannot readily be overheard so that each pair may work relatively undisturbed and uninhibited.

   C. The process
      1. The leader introduces the goals of the exercise. He indicates that it is often difficult in family life or group situations to spontaneously give or receive praise, constructive criticism, or negative responses to what happens. Why? Because most people do not want to interfere, to alienate others, or to be seen as troublemakers. Further, they don't know how others will respond. The purpose of this activity is to provide participants with an opportunity to pair off and exchange information about each other and to respond to the information they receive.
      2. Phase 1 of the activity: Data Gathering. Each participant pairs off

1. Adaptation of a structured experience "I Hear That You . . . : Giving and Receiving Feedback," by J. William Pfeiffer and John E. Jones, from *Annotated Handbook for Group Facilitators, 1981* (pp. 54–55), University Associates Publishers, John E. Jones, J. Wiliam Pfeiffer, Marshall Sashkin, et al., editors. Used by permission.

in rounds with every other person in the circle grouping. During each round partners will have three to five minutes to exchange, in turn, responses they have for each other. Phase 1 guidelines are both posted and reviewed by the leader, as follows:

a) It is a good idea to begin with positive exchanges and work toward negative issues.

b) The listener's task is to practice active listening and to ask for clarification only when necessary.

c) Those designated as informers may either pass on comments they have heard from other sources (reported information) or give personal reactions to the listeners.

d) Personal responses to the listener must be "owned," i.e., identified as such.

e) All sources are to remain confidential, i.e., during Phase 2 the listener may say, "I have heard that I . . ." but may *not* say, "Jim told me that Fred said that I . . .".

Duration—up to 5 minutes

3. Phase 1 begins when pairs begin conversations. One is informer, the other is listener. Each participant has blank paper and a pencil, and each pair is positioned in the room so that it will not conflict with or hinder the work of other pairs.

4. After three minutes the pairs are instructed to reverse roles.

5. After another three minutes the exchange is completed and pairs are allowed another minute or so to make notes on the responses they received. Then they select new partners.

Duration, 3–5—up to 8 minutes

6. The process continues with the partners reversing roles until each member of the group has exchanged responses with at least four other group members. A total of five separate pairings will have been completed in this segment of the process.

7. The participants are then asked to review privately all the information they have received. A period of up to five minutes is provided for this purpose.

Duration, 6–7—up to 40 minutes (concludes phase 1)

8. Phase 2 of the activity: Responding. The small group leader indicates that each person will have up to three minutes to inform the group about his perceptions concerning the information given him about himself. It is stressed that this is the time to clarify issues, kill rumors, and reinforce accurate information. Sources are to remain confidentially withheld.

9. As a group, the participants constructively discuss new perceptions about the use of responding to improve family and group work situations, and ways in which responding is both given and received.

Duration, 8–9—up to 25 minutes

Time elapsed for exercise: ca. 70 minutes

BREAK

IV. Achieving goals 1 and 2 through a study of Scriptural references and through segments devoted to skill mastery sequence review as the various skills are explained and mastered.
   Small groups consider themes and skills as follows:

   A. Jesus' request, God's answer: On hearing and responding. John 11:1–46 (esp. vv. 41–43).

   B. On listening and learning. Deuteronomy 31:9–13.

   C. God Listens—He Hears You, All Right! 2 Samuel 22 (esp. v. 7).

   D. Relationships, ministry, and family. 2 Peter 2:11 to 4:6. Note family and Christian community accents.

   E. Summary and review of salient issues raised in the small group setting, discussion leaders recording major points raised.

V. Discussion about skills reviewed and practiced:

   A. attending

   B. active listening

   C. providing negative responses

   D. caring through respect for personhood

   E. perceiving others' ideas or feelings

   F. linking behavior to perceptions

   G. establishing favorable listening climate for better interpersonal communication
   (A–G represents a minimal number of skills which should have been reviewed)

   Duration, 4–5—up to 50 minutes

VI. Reconvening for plenary session review.
   Assigned leaders present resumès of group discussions and findings in summary review in a sixty- to seventy-second capsule.

VII. Preview of the next unit, next session, with goals and a brief glimpse at one or two highlights ahead.

VIII. Closing prayer and hymn.

   Duration, VI–VIII—up to 15 minutes

   Time elapsed for session: ca. 2 hours, 30 minutes

A Final Observation

The instructional plan for this session includes at least some time for review and preview, two very essential considerations. Whatever the individual situation or necessary adaptations, and although each of the fundamental issues may be geared to suit local preferences, the element of continuity in learning is so vital that it must not be overlooked, or taken for granted. For this reason a part of the outline (C, 4e and C,7) accounts for a deliberate, Janus-like observation point. It is better to run the risk of slightly overdoing in this respect. There is simply too

75961

much going on from week to week and the distractions too many, to afford the kind of time adult Christians can, or possibly would, invest in reviewing skills or practicing them. That makes each instructional moment quite important, and the need for mental handles like reviews and reminders imperative.

As far as the initial unit in the series envisioned is concerned, these two complimentary lessons are seen as an important starting point in building expertise and momentum on the strength of the understandings, skills, and attitudinal framework which set both course and its pace. There aren't too many worthwhile accomplishments ahead without these listening skills in place, and so they serve as worthy leaders in an approach to the development and practice of a Family-Life Skills Workshop.

11

Skill Mastery in an Institute Setting

The Royal Priesthood, an Involved Citizenry

Goals for the Institute

1. Exploring and understanding Christian involvement in community affairs and the political arena.
2. Understanding and developing selected citizenship skills that positively affect national, state, and local government.
3. Developing expertise in assisting agencies that serve people and enhance community life.

Introduction

The institute format presented in this final skill-mastery unit offers still another type of setting for training in skills. An institute is actually an extended series of meetings to provide authoritative instruction by qualified specialists. The format has potential, therefore, to assist the participants in gaining insight and knowledgeability, in acquiring skills and in reviewing, if not redefining attitudes. And, of course, there is another outstanding benefit, that of working with acknowledged leaders, professionals, or specialists in the fields they represent.

This initial session aims at grounding the participants in a Scriptural approach to their responsibilities as Christians in the social, civic, and political aspects of their lives. The experts gathered to inform the institute will emphasize information from the New Testament, highlighting Pauline counsel on government and citizenship. The symposium presentation will set the stage for small group discussions on an outline that has been provided, detailing the major issues. During this period the participants will be alerted to, and begin thinking about, a voluntary pledge that will be made available in the final session.

The opening segment of the second session brings together, in a panel setting, a number of experts from various sectors of public life. The panel discussion will incorporate at least one specified skill that each public official on the panel seeks to bring to the insitute's attention. This will, in due time, prompt skill awareness and incentive during parts of the institute devoted to a number of selected skills and guided by the experts and additional trainers.

The institute is completed in the third session with one final study, in a forum arrangement, followed by a review and further practice of the institute skills. Finally, the pledge challenge to more active and purposeful Christian citizenship will be made available, but is not mandatory to any institute participant.

Setting, Arrangements, Learners, and Themes

This institute should probably be scheduled to take place some time after Labor Day, return-to-action time of the year in most parishes. Further, if offered during an election year, this institute is ideally suited to capitalize on the hectic action that usually takes the spotlight between Labor Day and Election Day. National, state, and local campaigns occupy attention at these times. But it is precisely during those times that it is well to refocus our attention on our responsibilities to neighbors, neighborhoods, and the citizens of our communities. For this reason, the institute features not only the political aspect of the Christian's life as a member of the state, but additionally, the social and community responsibilities closer to home as a member of both church and state.

In order to emphasize the dual aspect of Christian citizenship the site for such an institute should be a local church, and not a public facility. Bringing experts and officials *to* the church conveys very powerfully to all concerned, the priorities each has. On the one hand, the church demonstrates its interest in people and institutions. On the other hand, public officials and experts demonstrate their interest by participating and lending a hand to the informing process, thus underscoring their intention to assist in educating an alert and concerned citizenry.

Embedded in the internal arrangement of this institute are a number of presentations including a panel, a symposium, a forum, and group training sessions, as well as small group discussion units. Each of the principal figures will have to be selected, contacted, informed about individual responsibilities, and given appropriate directions. In an institute of this type it may be advisable to establish a registration fee, and it will undoubtedly be necessary to work with a central committee, which in turn may designate coordinators, group leaders, moderators, and the like. Whatever hospitality and instructional expenses may be involved, as well as accounting for these services from a personnel standpoint, will also be charged to fees, and under the guidance of designated leaders.

Of the skills outlined (see figure 4), these institute activities may be classified as adaptive skills inasmuch as they feature a capacity to shape, transform, or adjust to the various environments and spheres in which we live. Implicit in the wide range of activities envisioned in this institute are negotiating, regulating, making decisions, learning how to learn, adapting, and training, among others. The specific skills isolated for work during the institute in themselves contain still other skills.

You will want to note especially, that with the completion of this three-session institute we have had an opportunity to look at skill mastery in each of its aspects, i.e.: mental, adaptive, and interactive, and in a variety of units such as a typical instructional unit in a parish Bible class setting; a two-lesson unit as part of a workshop arrangement; and finally these three sessions, an institute setting emphasizing Christian citizenship responsibilities. Within each of the units presented there has been a variety of instructional activities, each of which was intended, in one way or another, to assist in skill development.

Once again, the learners, as must always be reiterated, are assumed to be concerned individuals who seek to participate in Kingdom building through the development or further advancement of the skills presented in this institute.

The over-arching theme of this institute, "The Royal Priesthood: An Involved Citizenry," is actually the banner on the masthead for each institute event. It is a theme that guides every session. Each session's goals tie into the institute theme in one way or another. Consequently, leaders and moderators will be responsible to coordinate all activities and outcomes around the general theme. Toward that end, it would be well to have a pictorial interpretation, overlayed with the theme caption, prominently displayed in a central gathering place, such as an auditorium or large meeting room at the institute site.

Institute Session 1

I. Welcome and Opening by the Institute Director

  A. Procedural matters, the institute schedule

  B. Explanation of small group designations, skill and information sessions

C. Welcome to groups and agencies sponsoring displays at various institute locations and booths

D. Introduction of symposium members, which include pastors of three local congregations

Duration—10 minutes

II. Symposium Presentation
The Royal Priesthood: Citizens of Two Kingdoms
Speaker 1   A Roman Citizen Speaks out on Good Government and Good Citizens (Rom. 13:1–7 and 1 Tim. 2:1–4)
Speaker 2   Calvin, Luther, and Pope Leo XIII: Perspectives on Church and State
Speaker 3   Contemporary Theological Accents on the Christian's Involvement in Community and Political Affairs

Note: A prepared abstract and outline for each presentation will be made available to each attendant.

Duration—35 minutes

III. Brief response period for clarification of terms, issues, and questions

Duration—10 minutes

IV. Assignments for followup mini-studies following the break
Pledge Alert: Toward Involved Christian Citizenship

Duration—5 minutes

BREAK

V. Followup Mini-Studies
Mini-studies will be directed by symposium members, assisted by appointed discussion leaders in sufficient numbers to enable assignment of groups of no more than ten members each. Symposium members rotate briefly to each group.
Mini-Study 1   Romans 13:1–7 and 1 Timothy 2:1–4
Mini-Study 2   Church, State, and the Christian Citizen: Historical Perspectives
Mini-Study 3   Church, State, and the Christian Citizen: Contemporary Perspectives

Duration—up to 1 hour

VI. Assembly for Session 1 Closing
Preview for Session 2 and Closing

Time elapsed for session: ca. 2 hours.

Institute Session 2

I. Welcome and Opening

A. Session 2 format and procedures

B. Instructions for participation

C. The pledge alert reminder

D. Introduction of panel guests

Duration—10 minutes

II. Panel Discussion
   Citizenship and Community Skills

   A. Panel members include:

   1. A state or federal government official, an elected member of the government

   2. A representative from the Women's League of Voters

   3. The director of the local United Way

   4. A representative from the Citizens' Advocate office

   5. The mayor or a representative of municipal government

   B. The panel moderator will lead a discussion, each panel member contributing:

   1. to the panel discussion on opportunities and challenges for effective Christian citizenship

   2. one specific political citizenship skill that will be explained and later practiced in workshop sessions

   Duration—10 minutes

   Note: Opportunities for questions and audience participation will be moderated by the panel leader.

III. Instructions for citizen skills workshop, display sites, and booths

   BREAK—up to 10 minutes

IV. Citizen Skills Workshops

   Five skill workshops conducted simultaneously, each institute attendant selecting one or more of the fifteen-minute presentations. Each presentation repeated three times to accommodate as many as possible.

   The demonstrations and workshops are designed to assist the institute participants in mastering contact, referral, communication, and organization skills involving various segments of social and political activity. At each display area or booth at least one of the several skills available may be studied and practiced according to the basic skill mastery taxonomy (figure 3).

   A. State or local government representative

   1. how to contact government representatives

   2. party and campaign organization

   3. governmental services

   4. running for public office

   B. Women's League of Voters representative

   1. getting helpful information

   2. voting rights and privileges

   3. registration procedures

   4. League of Women's Voters' projects

        5. knowing your political system

   C. United Way representative

        1. community services

        2. sources of help, types of help

        3. safety and disaster services

        4. family and youth services

   D. Citizens' Advocate representative

        1. advocacy and city services

        2. sources of help

        3. enforcement of city laws

   E. Municipal government representative

        1. mayoral/municipal offices

        2. basic municipal services

        3. caring for the elderly and other humanitarian services

        4. running for municipal office

        5. interest groups and city government

       Duration—up to 1 hour.

V. Assembly for Session 2 Closing
Preview for Session 3 and Closing

   Time Elapsed for Session: ca. 2 hours

Institute Session 3

  I. Welcome and Opening

    A. Session 3 format and participation instructions

    B. Pledge challenge review

    Duration—10 minutes

 II. Institute Forum
The Royal Priesthood: Concerned Citizens
    A study of two contemporary social issues and the involvement of Christian citizens as concerned and helpful people
    Assisting in the Forum discussion, with appropriate visual displays, is a professional team consisting of two pastors, two medical doctors, a registered nurse, and a Christian psychiatrist.
    The forum structure enables the moderator to introduce two subjects:

    A. drugs and drug abuse; and

    B. selected right-to-life issues.
        The discussion explores the issues, Biblical counsel, information presented by the gathered professionals, and presents both factual and ethical dimensions.

    Duration—up to 70 minutes

    BREAK

III. Skills review, with additional skills for dealing with drug abuse and right-to-life issues. Displays are available once again at the sites for skill practice. Each area has designated trainers, reviewing each session's skills.

IV. The Pledge Challenge

At reconvening for the final plenary session, the institute moves into its last official presentations. Participants are given the opportunity of signing a pledge card to be posted at local congregations, indicating their willingness to be of service, on call, or to volunteer for community action in the capacities featured in the institute program. The pledge is a voluntary commitment, not mandatory.

V. Distribution of Institute Certificates

Each participant who has attended all three institute sessions is awarded a certificate of successful participation.

Duration III–V—up to 1 hour

VI. Closing
The institute is closed with a prayer and the Doxology.

Time elapsed for session: ca. 2 hours, 20 minutes

A Final Observation

Both format and subject selection for these skill mastery activities have been chosen with an eye toward timeliness and a variety of style for adult Christian education. First, with regard to subject matter, the three areas of skill mastery are represented: mental, adaptive, and interactive. Topics have included Biblical interpretation, attentive listening, and a variety of social and policital skills. Second, concerning the format, there have been a number of structures presented, each intended to serve specific purposes, as well as to underscore their usefulness in skill mastery situations designed for adult learners.

A word or two about the various formats used in this institute's structure: each of the sessions contains a special form of presentation. They include a *symposium*, which is a series of related speeches by authorities or specialists qualified to speak on a given subject; a *panel*, which is an up-front discussion among three to six experts on an assigned topic; and a *forum*, which affords an opportunity to discuss, for a given period of time, one or two topics of interest that may be moderated and carried on by an entire group of people (the institute participants and the experts gathered for the session).

There is no doubt that institutes and presentations such as those here outlined take plenty of old-fashioned work, organization, and attention to many details. *But it's worth it!* Such arrangements are definitely *not out of the reach of typical church groups.* They provide stimulating change from the familiar routines we so often settle into, and they provide us with the kinds of exposures we all need to maintain a realistic contact with the social structures, agencies, and institutions that play such important roles in our lives. Isn't that reason enough to study them from a Biblical perspective? The New Testament contains persuasive evidence for just that very contention.

Part

A Slice of Life Under Study
The Case Study

The last of the three major approaches to adult settings in Christian education considered in these pages is by no means the least. In the case study we have a strategy that can be absorbing, challenging, capable of sharpening skills and redefining attitudes, and extremely helpful to us as individuals, and as members of a communion dedicated to the building of Christ's kingdom.

This particular approach to Christian education may incorporate still other strategies within its structure such as simulations and role-play vignettes (among many others), thus marking it off as one of the most versatile strategies available for profitable study at the adult level.

We will probe the Case Study differently. In the lecture-discussion and skill-mastery studies we followed a uniform pattern of approach to each. The outlines, explanations, and examples were similarly presented. Our examination of the case study, its nature and process, will address the same issues previously considered (the strategy, participant responsibilities, and the instructional task), but the alignment of material and the explanations will take on a different look with a substantially altered format.

As we look at the case study, we will consider still another possibility for use at the adult level of Christian education.

12

Potentials and Process

A case study contains information about an actual or hypo-thetical situation. It has been aptly called a slice of life. One or a number of problems are inherent in the study, and that makes it an excellent vehicle for the teaching-learning process, particularly in the areas of priority selection, the development of adaptive and interactive skills, and for confirming or redefining personal value structures.[1] Studies of this type require analyzing and evaluating the information presented so that, on the basis of applicable principles, recommendations for appropriate solutions or decisions may be made.

If you are looking for ways and means to bring problems, experiences, or the issues of everyday life right into the middle of an educational situation, the case study is a peerless choice. And if that slice of life needs a parallel reference point, the Bible is an equally superior choice. So I contend at the very outset that case studies are ideally suited for Bible class use, and further, that the Scriptures contain an almost inexhaustible supply of scenarios that qualify as case studies. Nor should we lose sight of the fact that this approach fulfills almost every conceivable requirement for the effective and edifying education of Christian adults. A review of figure 2, which details some of the essential requirements, will no doubt recall the superior ratings given in the case study. Indeed, as far as adult educational strategies go, this one stands out.

---

1. Leaders and teachers will want to make a special note of the fact that one of the three domains or divisions of learning, the affective domain, is best taught by comparing, analyzing, and developing value structures. Priority selection and the prioritizing of choices or decisions are major concerns in this regard. See Appendix D for more helpful information about the affective dimension (also known as the attitude domain) of the educational process.

For this reason we will examine its component parts, structure, and strengths before turning our attention to particular studies.

Until recently the case study has been the rather exclusive property of the helping professions. Social work—where the case history and its subsequent studies originated—medicine, and psychiatry, among others, have made extensive use of the case study for both diagnostic and instructional purposes. Of late, educators, too, have begun to turn to this strategy in ever greater numbers, increasingly aware that its versatility commends it for a variety of instructional uses.

The addition of this approach to adult instruction has resulted in impressive gains on both ends of the teaching-learning situation. The choice has been most fortunate because the case study offers a chance to learn through active participation by means of the opportunities it affords to bring personal experience to bear on the problem solving and decision making processes, and through the comparisons people and groups make with one another as they struggle with the cases presented. This combination of factors is made to order for adults in Bible class settings.

Since its introduction as a study vehicle, at the turn of the century, the number of case study types has proliferated, each variation aimed at differing aspects of diagnosis, decision making, character study, ethics, or problem solving. Additionally, these study types may contain still other processes or exercises. Further on we will examine a case study model outline which will serve as the primary format for the studies to follow. Each is similarly developed so that the uniformity of the cases will enable users to master a basic approach before venturing on to some of the variations currently in use.

You have no doubt noticed that problem solving and decision making skills have been mentioned time and again in connection with the case study. These two skills stand front and center in any strategy involving case studies. But there are others, including analyzing information, evaluating processes and ideas, isolating crucial or influential information, organizing resources, and using communicative skills. Add to these the necessary skills in interpersonal relationships requisite for cooperatively productive work, and you get some idea of the scope of this strategy's demands for skill, scholarship, and overall educational potential. It all adds up to an educational strategy of high intellectual demand, capable of using experience, stetching minds, and developing skills that may be called on time and again in everyday life. And there is an added bonus. Those who benefit from working through these case studies begin to develop their capabilities as maturing Christians who more effectively build Christ's kingdom.

Two considerations claim our attention as we prepare to use the case study. (1) The context for learning along with the instructional sequence of activities, and (2) the capabilities our participants will need for effective use of this strategy. We will obviously have to keep in mind the skills needed by the participants, nor should we lose sight of those special capabilities instructors must bring to this situation, such as helping with the procedures involved, setting the goals to be achieved, formulating the plan of action, and finally, providing ways and means to assess what has been done.

To begin with the participants: We have noted earlier that problem solving is at the very core of this strategy, and is a skill all should review and be able to use. Most of us have problem-solving patterns we have used with varying degrees of success. In order to standardize that approach for this particular case study situation, however, it might be well to outline the pattern best suited to this strategy.

1. We analyze the case as given for the purpose of defining exactly what we think the problem or series of problems may be.
2. Next we attempt to organize the information, evaluating its characteristics as we go, from the perspective of its bearing on the case. Notations will be necessary so that key people and their roles in the case, the sequence of events, and some reactions to the problem may be recorded.
3. A give-and-take discussion about some of the principles involved, relationships between personal experience and the case, and suggestions as to possible approaches, then takes place.[2]
4. Should the case be "live," requiring action on the basis of the decisions made, a final step would include an assessment of the action routes selected and the subsequent effect. Finally, an evaluation would be conducted.

Beyond problem-solving skills, participants will also be called upon to use group work skills, Biblical and referencing skills, discussion and consensus-making skills, plus a number of mental skills, especially those involving diagnosis, application, discrimination, and organization. Though too much taken for granted, these skills are essential and enter into each case studied. Cumulatively, they all have something to say about the

---

2. *Note:* At this point the case might well be concluded. If so, the participants have profited from the study through the discussion and a review of the possible applications to situations they themselves might encounter. Evaluation then brings the study to an end.

effectiveness of individual and collective coping abilities. Coping is taken here to mean the ability to deal with the problems, challenges, and responsibilities we as Christian adults face day in and day out. That is the bottom line for responsible adulthood. If, in some modest, constructive way, we can assist in the development of such skills and capabilities, put our experience to work, and draw on our Biblical knowledge to inform and guide us, we will indeed have taken some significant, positive steps toward the goal of equipping the saints.

As we turn to the concerns of the instructional process, we will concentrate primarily on the components of a typical session plan. Two are singled out: context and the sequence of instruction. The other two, stating the learning goals and evaluating progress, though equally important, will be treated as parts of the sequence itself.

Regarding the context, when the time comes, those much-needed outlines, folders, handouts, places for small groups to meet, and other resources, should be handy and ready to go. That is largely an organizational matter, but decisively important in the flow of instruction. It is best to leave no stone unturned in this respect. The other part of context, which has to do with an acquaintance and working knowledge of the people doing the study, is yet another matter. Knowing something more than names or faces is crucial to the process of selecting timely, helpful case studies for a given group's consideration. Instructors, therefore, will want to work out these two contextual factors quite carefully in anticipation of planning the work ahead.

There remains the challenge of developing an instructional plan for these slice-of-life studies. The number and extent of the variables involved suggest that this challenge is a formidable one and that it can be met successfully only if careful planning, resourceful use of facilities, materials, and personnel, and attention to detail are kept in mind as the planning is done. The following variables are especially noteworthy: (a) the type, complexity, and emotional intensity of the case under consideration; (b) what instructors and participants hope to achieve through the study; and (c) how the case study sessions are organized and conducted. For this reason, we will look at a case study model and examine its features in the hope that this prototype will be helpful in our planning.

Following the model outline, a number of case studies are presented. In each instance the case itself, along with the guidelines and outline material, is provided. The purpose of this structure, which will appear to be rather loose in comparison to the plans previously outlined, is to guide, but not inhibit planning on the local scene. It allows for whatever adaptations or additions may seem necessary at that level. Each case, finally, is subject to individual interpretation, and each is approached and studied according to the unique circumstances of a given group. So, once the background, procedure, and basic outline have been presented, the real work of studying the case is ready to begin.

13

A Case Study Sampler
The Great Deception

Devotional Opening

The Bible class may open this case study session with a devotional study of Psalm 37, concentrating especially on verses 22–29, which assure Christians of their blessed inheritance in the Lord. Appropriate hymns and prayers may be selected to enhance the devotion.

Case Description

Note: This part of the outline may be made available to Bible class members in the form of a prepared handout.

The Great Deception is an account of significant moments in the lives of Isaac, his wife Rebekah, and their twin sons Esau and Jacob. This particular set of events covers almost three full chapters in Genesis (25–28), which is as detailed and complete as Biblical coverage is likely to be. As we read through these chapters a number of major issues in the well-known story are revealed to us. These can be divided into three sections.

Case Outline

I. The Family of Isaac

  A. Esau is the first born of Rebekah's twin sons, and Jacob the second (Gen. 25:25–26).

    B. Isaac the father was partial to Esau, and Rebekah to Jacob (25:28).

    C. Genesis 25:23–26 describes a special reason for the birth of the twin brothers and the special relationship that existed between them.

  II. Birthright, Inheritance, and the Last Will and Testament

    A. Already in Genesis 15 we have an account of the manner in which an inheritance is to be passed from generation to generation (v. 2–5).

    B. Esau is to receive the inheritance by birthright, but he has already sold it (25:33–34), only to have the bargain struck over the birthright come back to haunt him (27:34–40).

  III. Deceptions and Guilt-Stained Gains

    A. The elderly Isaac seeks to give his blessing according to the accustomed manner (27:1–4).

    B. Rebekah's plot and Jacob's complicity subvert Isaac's intention (27:5–17).

    C. The Great Deception was, at any rate, an unnecessary subterfuge (25:22–23).

    D. Isaac blesses Jacob (27:18–29).

    E. A multitude of consequences begin to unfold (27:30 on through the next chapters).

Discussion Questions

1. What were the events in this account that had greatest influence on actions and outcomes? List them and prioritize them according to most decisive consequences.

2. What is your understanding of the meaning of the commandment: "Thou shalt not take the name of the Lord thy God in vain; for the Lord will not hold him guiltless that taketh his name in vain" (Exod. 20:7)? How does this understanding affect your estimation of the principal events in this case study?

3. Beside the principle just outlined in number 2, which other principles guide your consideration and judgment of the events in the Esau-Jacob account? Which do you think are most important C,

4. What is the direction of *my* daily choices? How would *I* respond to these further queries: Is the *now* so important that I would trade it away for *then* despite the principles involved? What might tempt me to do that very thing? In what respect am I like Esau? Like Jacob? List a number of situations that parallel the events of the case study. How would you react to them?

5. It was Sir Walter Scott who said, "O, what a tangled web we weave, When first we practice to deceive." Can you trace the truth of those lines through its tortuous route in the Genesis chapters under consideration?

Guidelines for Studying the Case in Small Groups

1. Use the outline, referring to the Biblical sections as a resource in isolating the critical features of the case study.

2. Use the case study questions to assist in your probe. Add those that seem important to you and your group beyond those listed.

3. Using the outline, resources, and the major problems or situations your small group (no more than ten people) has isolated, determine what your goals for discussion will be. You may want to consider: (a) goals about understanding the events, process, and problems in the case study, as well as those principles against which your group's judgments will be made; (b) goals involving applications for daily living; (c) goals examining attitudes and value structures, probing for reexamination, reassurance, and possible altering of present practices or habits; and (d) goals featuring applications, conclusions, and decisions on the basis of studying the Great Deception.

4. Develop a summary report to share with other small groups. This report is usually requested in the final, plenary session of the entire Bible class, assembled for its concluding activities.

Guidelines for Plenary Sessions

Bible classes may well choose to open and close their sessions as a group or as a collection of several study groups, affording an opportunity for the smaller units to compare findings with other groupings. These are very important, and the time spent in discussion of these reports can equal that given over to small group work. Equally important is the number and quality of the decisions, solutions, and applications proposed. Just how timely, influential, and conducive all this is to spiritual growth will be determined, and soon, on the basis of the skills, understandings, and dedication Bible class members bring to their responsibilities in daily living. That makes concluding summaries crucial, and a purposeful use of time is important during this segment of the case study session. The final part of this plenary closing should be guided by readings, hymns, and prayers that are as pertinent as those of the opening worship services.

A Concluding Comment

In most case studies there is a dominant issue or problem. True, there may be a cluster of variables or additional circumstances to complicate matters, but there is usually a root cause, or problem, that sets the stage and provides the momentum for the events taking place in these mini-dramas. The instructional challenge is to get down to the nub of the problem, to suggest practical and ethically defensible ways and means to solve it, and to apply those solutions to everyday, Christ-centered living.

The Great Deception does not depart from this typical mold. The problem is actually quite near the surface, so easily recognizable, and in so many respects quite blatantly self-centered, that it almost seems unworthy of mature consideration. And yet, there are those telltale evidences of flawed character we recognize only too well, which mark it off as a classic study in human frailty. It is the kind of scenario enacted in our own lives far too often. As a matter of plain fact, we really need to study this case quite carefully.

The Great Deception has been outlined as a model case study taken diectly from the Scriptures, and the plot line was followed closely, with only a reference or two from additional sources in Genesis to round out a fuller meaning. That procedure follows the usual case study approach, which endeavors to present the issues without bias and in a straightforward sequence. The studies that follow, though not as completely detailed, are based on a number of Old Testament, New Testament, and contemporary cases. These cases follow the same general procedure, challenging both teachers and participants to use the cases as best suits local circumstances or situations. Before turning to those studies, we pause to review, in sequential order, the outline used for these studies:

1. *The case description:* Presented on a one-page handout in narrative or outline form.

2. *Study of the case description:* Participants determine the salient issues, variables, and facts and prioritize them as to the most influential; it is helpful at this point is to recall situations similar to the case itself as a comparison with everyday experience.

3. *Statement of case study intentions:* Participants state what their goals will be with regard to the case and to its application in their lives.

4. *Evaluation of the information presented:* Discussions about the case and the guideline questions lead the participants toward approaches to solutions or suggested remedial actions in line with stated goals.

5. *Comparisons:* If more than one group studies the same case, comparisons of discussions and approaches are made, and ethical dimensions are reviewed on the basis of the principles used to guide choices and priorities. At this point a final decision may be made or a consensus achieved.

6. *Case review:* An optional, but worthwhile step—the case review will be a necessary final step, particularly if action follows the case study; in that case the participants will review their solutions and actions in terms of their goals and of the principles which guided their activity.

14

Twelve Old Testament Case Studies

Did He Really Say That?
Genesis 3:1–13

Case Study Outline

I. The Serpent/Satan tempts God's own (vv. 1–7).

II. Temptation's allure and the fall (vv. 6–8).

III. The accounting (vv. 9–13).

    A. Man's problem

    B. Satan's problem

Case Description

(Recording of Genesis 3:1–13)

A Comparable Scriptural Reference

Romans 5:12–21

Issues and Problems Raised

1. Trusting and doubting are two fundamental factors involved in every relationship. How do they affect the relationships and the decisions we make?

FIGURE 8 **Sample Case Study Layout**

Did He Really Say That?
Genesis 3:1–13

Case Study Outline

I. The Serpent/Satan tempts God's own (vv. 1–7).
II. Temptation's allure and the fall (vv. 6–8).
III. The accounting (vv. 9–13).
   A. Man's problem
   B. Satan's problem

12 And the man said, The woman whom thou gavest *to be* with me, she gave me of the tree, and I did eat.
13 And the Lord God said unto the woman, What *is* this *that* thou hast done? And the woman said, The serpent beguiled me, and I did eat.

A Comparable Scriptural Reference

Romans 5:12–21

Case Description

Now the serpent was more subtil than any beast of the field which the Lord God had made. And he said unto the woman, Yea, hath God said, Ye shall not eat of every tree of the garden?
2 And the woman said unto the serpent, We may eat of the fruit of the trees of the garden:
3 But of the fruit of the tree which *is* in the midst of the garden, God hath said, Ye shall not eat of it, neither shall ye touch it, lest ye die.
4 And the serpent said unto the woman, Ye shall not surely die:
5 For God doth know that in the day ye eat thereof, then your eyes shall be opened, and ye shall be as gods, knowing good and evil.
6 And when the woman saw that the tree *was* good for food, and that it *was* pleasant to the eyes, and a tree to be desired to make *one* wise, she took of the fruit thereof, and did eat, and gave also unto her husband with her; and he did eat.
7 And the eyes of them both were opened, and they knew that they *were* naked; and they sewed fig leaves together, and made themselves aprons.
8 And they heard the voice of the Lord God walking in the garden in the cool of the day: and Ăd′ăm and his wife hid themselves from the presence of the Lord God amongst the trees of the garden.
9 And the Lord God called unto Ăd′ăm, and said unto him, Where *art* thou?
10 And he said, I heard thy voice in the garden, and I was afraid, because I *was* naked; and I hid myself.
11 And he said, Who told thee that thou *wast* naked? Hast thou eaten of the tree, whereof I commanded thee that thou shouldest not eat?

Issues and Problems Raised

1. Trusting and doubting are two fundamental factors involved in every relationship. How do they affect the relationships and the decisions we make?

2. _____
_____

3. _____
_____

A Contemporary Situation Suggested by This Case

Statement of Intent

1. We will examine some of the effects doubts have on our relationship with God and with other Christians.

2. _____
_____

3. _____
_____

The Principles Governing Our Judgments and Decisions

1. We accept God's Word as the truth. Such an acceptance should affect every decision we make.

2. _____

_____

3. _____

_____

4. _____

_____

Discussion Questions

1. How does a reasonable-sounding promise of wealth or notoriety affect our thinking and, subsequently, our relationships with others?

2. _____

_____

3. _____

_____

4. _____

_____

5. _____

Decisions and Suggested Solutions

Case Review: An Assignment

A Contemporary Situation Suggested by This Case

Statement of Intent

1. We will examine some of the effects doubts have on our relationship with God and with other Christians.

The Principles Governing Our Judgments and Decisions

1. We accept God's Word as the truth. Such an acceptance should affect every decision we make.

Discussion Questions

1. How does a reasonable-sounding promise of wealth or notoriety affect our thinking and, subsequently, our relationships with others?

Decisions and Suggested Solutions

Case Review: An Assessment

Constrained
Genesis 39:1–19

Case Study Outline

I. Joseph, having been sold into slavery by his brothers, is brought to Egypt to serve the Egyptian Pharaoh's chief officer, Potiphar (v. 1).

II. Under God's blessing, Joseph renders outstanding service (vv. 2–6).

III. Potiphar's wife, attracted to Joseph, boldly offers herself to him (vv. 7–8).

IV. Joseph: How can I do this great wickedness and sin against God? (v. 9).

V. Undaunted, Potiphar's wife renews her efforts, tempting Joseph again and again (vv. 10–13).

VI. Joseph's refusals frustrate Potiphar's wife, and she plots against him, creating a dilemma for Potiphar as well as problems for Joseph (vv. 14–19).

Case Description

(Recording of Genesis 39:1–19)

A Comparable Scriptural Reference

Ephesians 5:1–17

Issues and Problems Raised

1. When we perceive real and present danger to name, welfare, or health, we react promptly. Is our reaction principled or a response of expedience?

A Contemporary Situation Suggested by this Case

Statement of Intent

1. We will attempt to determine what an equitable and God-pleasing response to a situation such as the one which Potiphar encountered, might be.

The Principles Governing Our Judgments and Decisions

1. Speaking the truth in love may at times be excruciatingly difficult, but it is always, and without exception, the way God would have it done.

Discussion Questions

1. In 1 Corinthians 10:13 Paul speaks to all Christians about resisting and escaping temptation. What does will power have to do with escaping temptation, and what are the ways it can be nourished?

Decisions and Suggested Solutions

Case Review: An Assessment

We're Going to Do This *Our* Way
Exodus 32:1–6

Case Study Outline

I. Moses' absence from the Israelite encampment sets the stage for apostasy (v. 1).

II. Aaron, the man in charge during Moses' absence, is an easy mark for the grumbling Israelites; he does not even hesitate in yielding to their demand (v. 2).

III. The golden calf is built; all contribute (vv. 3–4).

IV. An altar is built before the calf (v. 5).

V. A calf-worship festivity commences (v. 6).

Case Description

(Recording of Exodus 32:1–6)

A Comparable Scriptural Reference

Acts 17:1–23

Issues and Problems Raised

1. The problem of effective leadership for God's people was a constant source of concern. An astonishingly low percentage of people seems to be cut

out for leadership. An astonishingly high percentage of mankind seems capable only of grumbling and half-hearted loyalty. Moses, Aaron, and the Israelites provide examples of each. The problem: How to overcome these weaknesses?

A Contemporary Situation Suggested by This Case

Statement of Intent

1. We will try to determine the responsibilities of leadership Aaron might have demonstrated in Moses' absence.

The Principles Governing Our Judgments and Decisions

1. It was a scant few days prior to this incident that this principle was given: "Thou shalt have no other gods before me. Thou shalt not make unto thee any graven image, or any likeness of any thing that is in heaven above, or that is in the earth beneath, or that is in the water under the earth." (Exod. 20: 3–4).

Discussion Questions

1. Rising against a popular tide is at best a hazardous undertaking. What measures and alternatives are advisable?

Decisions and Suggested Solutions

Case Review: An Assessment

At Great Risk
Joshua 2:1–24

Case Study Outline

I. Two of Joshua's handpicked advance men are sent to spy in the kingdom of Jericho before the Israelites attempt to take it (v. 1).

II. The two men encounter difficulties, but Rahab, risking her own life as well as the lives of her family members, hides them, going so far as to conceal them and to divert those in search of the two spies (vv. 2–7).

III. Rahab, recently converted, a prostitute, covenants with the spies for the safety of her family. An agreement is made and instructions follow (vv. 8–21).

IV. The spies return to Joshua and make their report (vv. 22–24).

Case Description

(Recording of Joshua 2:1–24)

A Comparable Scriptural Reference

1 Corinthians 4:9–14

Issues and Problems Raised

1. Spying is risky business. Harboring spies is even riskier. It amounts to treason, an offense punishable by death. Trust among people caught in such a web is achievable only at great expense amid wariness and discomfort. The problem: How much of a risk is acceptable and what kind of stakes prompt such risks?

A Contemporary Situation Suggested by This Case

Statement of Intent

1. We would like to examine the relationship between risk and trust, and between our convictions, hopes, and the extent or limits of an acceptable risk.

The Principles Governing Our Judgments and Decisions

1. A covenant is basically a trust relationship, broken already when that trust is in any way betrayed. Subsequent penalty or loss is the result, not a part of the actual essence of a covenant.

Discussion Questions

1. Note how God uses apparently unsavory people and apparently devious means to accomplish His purpose. Would the right question be: Do the ends, after all, justify the means? How would you justify your response?

Decisions and Suggested Solutions

Case Review: An Assessment

You Are the One!
2 Samuel 12:1–12

Case Study Outline

I. God sends Nathan, the prophet who counseled both Solomon and David, to speak to King David after the events of the David-Bathsheba love affair had transpired (v. 1).

II. Nathan confronts David with a parable and the king reacts with disgust, passing judgment on the incident exactly as God, through Nathan, intended him to see it (vv. 2–6).

III. Nathan lays bare David's sin: "You are the one" (vv. 7–12).

Case Description

(Recording of 2 Samuel 12:1–12)

A Comparable Scriptural Reference

Acts 4:1–12

Issues and Problems Raised

1. Nathan's problem is often our problem: confronting people of great authority with their weaknesses, limitations, ineptitudes, or sinfulness. How do we dare do it, and how is it to be done?

A Contemporary Situation Suggested by This Case

1. We would like to determine an appropriate and God-pleasing approach to the difficulties involved in constructive criticism.

The Principles Governing Our Judgments and Decisions

1. Analysis, critical judgment, and correction are important responsibilities in the lives of Christians. It is done with the upbuilding and welfare of the recipient foremost in mind.

Discussion Questions

1. What do you think of Nathan's parabolic approach to his difficult assignment? Under which circumstances would you consider this to be a strategically sound approach?

Decisions and Suggested Solutions

Case Review: An Assessment

On the Spot
1 Kings 18:1–20

Case Study Description

I. Elijah, who was God's prophet during the reign of the Israelite King Ahab, is sent by God to tell the king a rainstorm will break a drought and famine that had hit the kingdom hard (vv. 1–2).

II. Ahab had previously sent Obadiah, one of his high ranking officers (later a prophet), in search of food and resources for his military, people, and horses (vv. 3–6).

III. Obadiah encounters Elijah and soon finds himself positioned between two powerful and contending forces. He is confronted with having to return to Ahab with news that will undoubtedly outrage him (vv. 7–13).

IV. Obadiah carries out the mission Elijah gives him. There are surprising results (vv. 14–20).

Case Description

(Recording of 1 Kings 18:1–20)

A Comparable Scriptural Reference

(1 Samuel 17:1–58)

Issues and Problems Raised

1. Caught between a rock and a hard place is a common saying based on situations common to most of us. We seem to be unable to succeed no matter what our choice. The issue at stake: What is the compelling force, finally, that moves us to act?

A Contemporary Situation Suggested by This Case

Statement of Intent

1. We would like to agree on some guidelines, based on these Scriptures, which will be helpful in our decision-making processes.

The Principles Governing Our Judgments and Decisions

1. Even in the most desperate of situations God uses His own means to achieve His purposes and will not fail to comfort those who believe in Him.

Discussion Questions

1. In what ways does the experience of the Israelites, and that of Obadiah, remind us that the nature and circumstances of mankind do not change?

Decisions and Suggested Solutions

Case Review: An Assessment

Treachery Has Its Own Reward
Judges 16:4–16 and 19–31

Case Study Outline

I. Samson falls in love with Delilah, the Philistine beauty (v. 4).

II. Delilah's people persuade her to discover the secret of Samson's strength and attempt to overpower him. Each time Samson deceives them and they fail (vv. 5–14).

III. Delilah persists, reproaching Samson for his deceit and mockery (vv. 15–16).

IV. The treachery perpetrated on all sides has consequences for all involved (vv. 19–31).

Case Description

(Recording of Judges 16:4–16 and 19–31)

A Comparable Scriptural Reference

Matthew 26:47–50

Issues and Problems Raised

1. The trade-off is part and parcel of family, work, and social life. It is often a problem to know what makes a trade-off beneficial and whether it can be accomplished with integrity. In fact, in these situations we are often faced with real and perplexing dilemmas.

A Contemporary Situation Suggested by This Case

Statement of Intent

1. Bible class members will examine the sequence of events and the salient issues in the Biblical account to determine and understand, according to their perceptions, at least two or three of the issues or problems raised.

The Principles Governing Our Judgments and Decisions

1. Sin can be overpowering, stampeding conscience and insistently prompting us to set aside both God and fellows in order to satisfy ourselves. God's law shows us our sin and stands ready to warn us about the nature and consequence of its destructive power.

Discussion Questions

1. What are some of the constructive and destructive dimensions of power? How do we deal with power from the perspective of either having it, or of not having it?

Decisions and Suggested Solutions

Case Review: An Assessment

Not Without Trouble
Ezra 4:1–24

Case Study Outline

Introduction: Ezra, one of the truly great men of Israelite history, had received letters of certification and approval to begin building the Temple.

I. The Israelites begin building the Temple (v. 1).

II. Permission to assist in the building, which would join the Samaritans and other people to the Israelites, is requested by the Samaritans (v. 2).

III. Zerubbabel and Jeshua, leaders of the Israelites, deny the request (II Kings 17 presents background for their decision) (v. 3).

IV. The building goes on, but not without trouble (vv. 4–5).

V. Finally, the building of both the Temple and the city wall is halted altogether through a combination of threats, intrigue, and political maneuvering (vv. 6–24).

Case Description

(Recording of Ezra 4:1–24)

A Comparable Scriptural Reference

Luke 14:25–33

Issues and Problems Raised

1. Confronted with an offer from people who probably meant well, at least at the outset, the Israelites saw fit to reject it on theological grounds. At issue: Under what circumstances may we sanction work and worship with others?

A Contemporary Situation Suggested by This Case

Statement of Intent

1. Bible class members will examine Ezra 4:1–24 and Luke 14:25–33 to develop insights and understanding about the cost of discipleship and some of the consequences they might expect as the result of a determined stand on principle.

The Principles Governing Our Judgments and Decisions

1. "For which of you, intending to build a tower, sitteth not down first, and counteth the cost, whether he have sufficient to finish it?" (Luke 14:28).

Discussion Questions

1. Much is made of the ecumenical movement. What does the Ezra account tell us about ecumenism?

Decisions and Suggested Solutions

Case Review: An Assessment

A Golden Silence
Esther 2:1–20

Case Study Outline

I. Esther and Mordecai, her guardian, dominate the part of Israelite history (ca. 500 B.C.) contained in the book named after the Persian Queen. In the first section of chapter 2 the circumstances of the selection of a queen for King Ahasuerus are described verses 1–14.

II. Esther emerges as the king's favorite and his choice (vv. 15–16).

III. Esther is made the queen and a great ceremony marks the event. Celebrations follow (vv. 17–18).

IV. On Mordecai's advice Esther has not yet revealed to the king that she is a Jewess (vv. 19–20).

Case Description

(Recording of Esther 2:1–20)

A Comparable Scriptural Reference

Ephesians 6:10–13

Issues and Problems Raised

1. Sometimes silence *is* golden. The problem is often *when*, not *whether*, certain facts should be presented.

A Contemporary Situation Suggested by This Case

Statement of Intent

1. We would like to trace the development of the two heroes of the book of Esther to see how their faith affected their priorities and the decisions they made, as reported not only in chapter 2, but in the remainder of this short (10 chapters) and final historical book of the Old Testament.

The Principles Governing Our Judgments and Decisions

1. Wisdom and consideration guide our choice of the time and the place to share essential and critically important truths.

Discussion Questions

1. Sometimes the fate of an entire nation or people hangs on the thread of seemingly unimportant actions or events. How was this manifested in the history of the Israelite people as related through the story of Persia, Esther, and Mordecai?

Decisions and Suggested Solutions

Case Review: An Assessment

Convictions
Daniel 3:1–15

Case Study Outline

Introduction: Daniel and his three renamed friends, Shadrach, Meshach, and Abednego, holders of high office in the Babylonian Empire due to their special training, were already some twenty years deep into their service of King Nebuchadnezzar. Despite captivity in a land hostile to their God, and despite their favored high office, they remained faithful to their God throughout their years in Babylon.

I. King Nebuchadnezzar orders that an image of gold be struck, and that it must be worshiped (vv. 1–5).

II. The penalty for failure to worship the image is announced (vv. 6–7).

III. The Chaldeans inform the king that the Jews, particularly Shadrach, Meshach, and Abednego will not worship the golden image (vv. 8–12).

IV. Shadrach, Meshach, and Abednego are put to the test (vv. 13–15).

Case Description

(Recording of Daniel 3:1–15)

A Comparable Scriptural Reference

1 Peter 4:12–19

Issues and Problems Raised

1. The acid test, as we often call it, measures not only the depth of our convictions, but our resolve to act on those convictions.

A Contemporary Situation Suggested by This Case

Statement of Intent

1. We will examine this case in the light of our own commitment to (a) relatively harmless causes that call for little or no personal danger, and (b) life-threatening or otherwise endangering causes, to see how we might respond to such situations.

The Principles Governing Our Judgments and Decisions

1. Joshua's challenge and his example set the principle: "And if it seem evil unto you to serve the Lord, choose you this day whom ye will serve; whether

the gods which your fathers served that were on the other side of the flood, or the gods of the Amorites, in whose land ye dwell; but as for me and my house, we will serve the Lord" (Joshua 24:15).

Discussion Questions

1. If you have not been challenged to within an inch of your life, how will you prepare for that moment?

Decisions and Suggested Solutions

Case Review: An Assessment

On Deaf Ears
Amos 7:1–17

Case Study Outline

I. In the midst of prosperous times and unchallenged power, Amos, an unpretentious man of the soil, delivers a stunning warning in the form of three visions to the sophisticates of church and state (vv. 1–9). The third of these visions contains a doomsday forecast for Bethel, as well as for the Northern Kingdom (vv. 7–9).

II. The chief priest at Bethel, Amaziah, finds the blunt message of this coarse, unfinished country "priest" offensive and banishes Amos (vv. 10–13).

III. Undaunted, Amos stands his ground to deliver God's message, but it falls on disbelieving and deaf ears (vv. 14–17).

Case Description

(Recording of Amos 7:1–17)

A Comparable Scriptural Reference

Acts 7:37–53

Issues and Problems Raised

1. Training, credentials, experience, and rank are the marks of successful and influential people. A problem: Do such marks influence our judgment of what has been said or done so that it is measured not on the basis of its merit, but on the basis of the source?

A Contemporary Situation Suggested by This Case

Statement of Intent

1. We want to look closely at the circumstances that surround the

proclamation of God's judgment in order to understand the nature of a wise and just judgmental process.

The Principles Governing Our Judgments and Decisions

1. Our assessment of any kind of proposal or suggestion should focus on its inherent merit.

Discussion Questions

1. What effective ways and means can you suggest to get through to people who seem to have deaf ears? At what point would you rest your case and say, That's it; I've had it?

Decisions and Suggested Solutions

Case Review: An Assessment

Despite Himself
Jonah 3:1–4:3

Case Study Outline

I. In the last two short chapters of this book Jonah reluctantly fulfills his missionary responsibilities witnessing to the Ninevehites, a scourge to the entire Mid-East region (3:1–3).

II. Despite Assyrian arrogance and Jonah's misgivings about the merit of such an apparently hopeless mission, the people heed the warnings of God's message delivered by Jonah (3:4–10).

III. This turn of events not only shocks a disbelieving Jonah, but displeases him, and he prays that God would strike down these people (4:1–3).

Case Description

(Recording of Jonah 3:1–4:3)

A Comparable Scriptural Reference

Luke 15: 28–32

Issues and Problems Raised

1. After being disappointed or angered over protracted disobedience or insubordination we find ourselves wary and mistrusting at the turning-over of a new leaf.

A Contemporary Situation Suggested by This Case

Statement of Intent

1. Bible class members will investigate the account from the perspective of (a) the outline of events as they transpired, (b) the factors that made these events seem improbable, and (c) personal reactions to the incredulity of Jonah in this situation.

The Principles Governing Our Judgments and Solutions

1. When God's purpose is accomplished there is cause for rejoicing; in such circumstances *Soli Deo Gloria* leaves no room for personal gratification or aggrandizement.

Discussion Questions

1. How can we equip God's people to be selfless servants and willing witnesses?

Decisions and Suggested Solutions

Case Review: An Assessment

15

Eight New Testament Case Studies

The Ultimate Contradiction
Matthew 12:22–37

Case Study Outline

Introduction: The confrontation between Jesus Christ and the Pharisees described in these verses is but one of the many contained in the Synoptic Gospels. This one, however, addresses the most crucial of all faith-life issues: the call to repentance, faith, and trust in Christ as personal Savior. To commit the unpardonable sin is to blaspheme against God's Spirit, viz., willfully rejecting Christ as personal Savior. That is, at bottom, what this fiercely heated exchange is all about.

I. The scenario is actually occasioned by Christ's miracle, the healing of a man possessed of the devil, who also happened to be blind (v. 22).

II. The people are amazed, but the Pharisees accuse Christ: He himself is using demonic power. That is an ultimate contradiction (vv. 23–30).

III. The unpardonable sin against the Holy Ghost (vv. 31–32).

IV. Every word counts; there is no idle word. Christ calls people to witness through word and deed (vv. 33–37).

Case Description

(Recording of Matthew 12:22–37)

A Comparable Scriptural Reference

Mark 3:22–30

Issues and Problems Raised

1. Turning truth upside down is as old as human history. Using truth as a strategic element in lying confuses people and tends to set them up for the ulterior motives of others. How can we guard against that?

A Contemporary Situation Suggested by This Case

Statement of Intent

1. Bible class members will list the facts they perceive to be the most influential in this event, in order to get at the motives, meanings, and purpose of this exchange between Christ and the Pharisees.

The Principles Governing Our Judgments and Solutions

1. There is no neutral ground in Kingdom building. We either represent and witness to Christ truthfully, thus building His kingdom, or we do not, thus scattering His kingdom.

Discussion Questions

1. If you were to encounter this kind of a situation, how do you think it would affect your faith? How do you think you would react?

Decisions and Suggested Solutions

Case Review: An Assessment

Murderous Entertainment
Mark 6:14–25

Case Study Outline

I. Many, including Herod Antipas, ruler over Galilee, wondered about the power of Jesus, His disciples, and about John the Baptizer. Herod recalled the manner in which he had done away with John the Baptist, due in large part to his sister-in-law, Herodias, even though he had formerly befriended him. But now his own birthday banquet set the stage for Herodias to gain revenge on the man who challenged her affair with Herod as adulterous and unacceptable (vv. 14–21).

II. The banquet festivities featured the dancing of Herodias's daughter Salome, who so charmed Herod that he vowed publicly to grant her any wish. Herodias seized that opportunity to instruct Salome to request the head of the imprisoned John the Baptist, which she did (vv. 22–25).

Case Description

(Recording of Mark 6:14–25)

A Comparable Scriptural Reference

Isaiah 65:11–14

Issues and Problems Raised

1. Note the twists and turns of people, events, and individual appetites. Herod, the governor of the territory no less, is himself caught in a tightening web. Several problems emerge involving Herod, Salome, and finally Herodias.

A Contemporary Situation Suggested by This Case

Statement of Intent

1. Bible class members will isolate critical factors in this account, prioritizing them as to their effect on final outcomes.

The Principles Governing Our Judgments and Solutions

1. Those without scruples of any kind will use means of any kind to accomplish their purposes.

Discussion Questions

1. As good as my word is an expression that indicates our determination to fulfill that which we promise. What lesson(s) does this account teach us about public proclamations and oaths?

Decisions and Suggested Solutions

Case Review: An Assessment

Not To Be Denied
Mark 10:46–52

Case Study Outline

I. The apostle Mark refers to the blind man at the city gate of Jericho as Bartimaeus. This man, on hearing that Jesus was leaving the city, insisted loudly that Jesus be brought to him (vv. 46–47).

II. During the several hours He had been in Jericho, Jesus' deeds stirred great interest, attracting many. The crowds gathered, following Him to the city gates. Hearing the clamor Bartimaeus raised, the people tried to shunt him aside, shushing him. That only caused Bartimaeus to become more insistent pleading his case directly to Jesus (vv. 48).

III. Jesus heard and responded (vv. 49–52).

Case Description

(Recording of Mark 10:46–52)

A Comparable Scriptural Reference

Matthew 15:21–28

Issues and Problems Raised

1. During His later Judean ministry, Jesus was confronted with a number of problems, similar to the one occasioned by Bartimaeus's plea. In this instance it is not only the blind man who presents a problem. The public ministry of Jesus called for an awareness of the high stakes involved; there were beneficiaries of His compassion, true, but there were always witnesses, some of whom were skeptical and hostile. A problem: Why should Jesus, on His way to Jerusalem, stop yet again to become involved over one, solitary person, a blind man?

A Contemporary Situation Suggested by This Case

Statement of Intent

1. We would like to examine our attitudes about those constant interruptions and how to deal with them.

The Principles Governing Our Judgments and Decisions

1. Where there is a will, there is a way is an expression of both faith and determination. When convinced we are in the right we move ahead with the determination of a Bartimaeus not to be denied.

Discussion Questions

1. How do our priorities affect our interpretation of events as to whether they are important, indifferent, or a nuisance?

Decisions and Suggested Solutions

Case Review: An Assessment

Obedience
Luke 2:41–52

Case Study Outline

Introduction: of the many possible topic choices available in Luke 2, Jesus' respect and obedience for elders, teachers, and His parents has been chosen. Verses 41–52 form the entire section; 41–48 set the stage, and 48–52 are the verses of prime consideration.

I. There is only one account of Jesus' life history between the flight of Joseph's family to Egypt and the beginning of His ministry: this appearance in the Temple at Jerusalem at the feast of the Passover (vv. 41–43).

II. Joseph and Mary search for their son, apparently lost, and their search ultimately leads them to the Temple where they are disturbed, yet relieved to find Him engaged in discussions with the teachers and Temple priests (vv. 44, 45–49).

III. Jesus answers His parents' questions and returns, as an obedient son, to Nazareth with them (vv. 50–52).

Case Description

(Recording of Luke 2:41–52)

A Comparable Scriptural Reference

1 Samuel 1–2.

Issues and Problems Raised

1. At first glance Jesus' reply to His mother's concerned inquiries seems less than respectful. Already at these early stages of budding youth Jesus' unique role as very God, yet very man, places Him in what seem to us as awkward positions. At issue is upholding the law of God, yet interpreting it in the light of the New Covenant relationship.

A Contemporary Situation Suggested by This Case

Statement of Intent

1. Bible class members will investigate, list, and discuss the responsibilities of parents and children on the basis of this narrative.

The Principles Governing Our Judgments and Decisions

1. The Christian family is organized around parental authority, respect, and reciprocal responsibilities, all of which are labors of love for each member of the family and for our heavenly Father.

Discussion Questions

1. What are some of the dimensions of Mary's role which come to light in this narrative?

Decisions and Suggested Solutions

Case Review: An Assessment

Número Uno?
Luke 9:37–48

Case Study Outline

I. During his Galilean ministry Jesus' disciples witnessed many evidences of his patience, power, and love. The healing of this epileptic lad is typical. It was prompted by the disciples' inability to deal with the father's request for healing—a most interesting aside, considering the scenario about to unfold (vv. 37–40).

II. Jesus responds both to the needs of the epileptic and his own disciples (vv. 41–43).

III. Jesus chastises the disciples. They have completely misinterpreted the import of these events, turning instead to heated discussions about who among them is in fact the greatest (vv. 44–46).

IV. Jesus sees quite plainly what the situation is and reacts as only He can and must (vv. 47–48).

Case Description

(Recording of Luke 9:37–48)

A Comparable Scriptural Reference

Matthew 20:17–28

Issues and Problems Raised

1. Who is number One? Who is the greatest? Who gets the highest reward? More often than not these are precisely the wrong questions. At issue here is our perception, resolve, and subsequent action according to rightly ordered priorities. The problem: How do we order priorities to avoid the disciples' drastic mistake?

A Contemporary Situation Suggested by This Case

Statement of Intent

1. On the basis of this account we would like to determine an acceptable course of action to pursue over against the possibility of becoming unnecessarily involved in counterproductive arguments.

The Principles Governing Our Judgments and Decisions

1. In serving Christ the principle involves this great paradox; "He that is least among you, the same shall be great" (Luke 9:48b).

Discussion Questions

1. Instead of the questions posed in Issues and Problems Raised (above), what questions might rather be raised about status, role, or purpose in serving Christ?

Decisions and Suggested Solutions

Case Review: An Assessment

People in Glass Houses
John 8:3–11

Case Study Outline

I. In another of a continuing series of confrontations with the Pharisees, Christ is faced with the issue of Mosaic law regarding the consequences of adultery (vv. 3–5).

II. Christ sets the stage for the well-known cast-the-first-stone challenge, which causes the accusers to leave, one by one, in silent acknowledgment of their own transgression (vv. 6–9).

III. Christ turns now to the young lady, challenging her to a new life dedicated to God (vv. 10–11).

Case Description

(Recording of John 8:3–11)

A Comparable Scriptural Reference

Romans 2:1–16

Issues and Problems Raised

1. Human nature being what it is, we find evidence almost daily to underscore the homespun truth implied in the old axiom, people in glass houses shouldn't throw stones. At issue is more than integrity. There is also a rather grudging acknowledgment that we are sinful and do indeed sin. Which other sayings shed similar light on this problem?

A Contemporary Situation Suggested by this Case

Statement of Intent

1. Bible class members will attempt to ascertain three implications of struggles such as this one between Jesus and the Pharisees, listing them according to rank, from the least to the greatest threat to our spiritual lives.

The Principles Governing Our Judgments and Decisions

1. Luther gives us a principle in his commentary on this section of John's Gospel: "This, then, is the difference between the Kingdom of Christ and the kingdom of the world, that Christ makes all men sinners. He does not let that be the end, but it follows that He absolves men."

Discussion Questions

1. What does this case study teach you about the actual content, the inferences, and the manner and style of the questions we are asked and about the responses we choose to make?

Decisions and Solutions Suggested

Case Review: An Assessment

Who Will Know the Difference?
Acts 5:1–11

Case Study Outline

I. Ananias and his wife, Sapphira, having sold a piece of property, withheld a percentage of the profit and presented the remainder to the church at Jerusalem (vv. 1–2).

II. It did not take very long for Peter to appear on the scene to inquire of Ananias what this donation was all about. Ananias, faithful to the deception he and his wife planned, lied to Peter about the transaction. He paid for that with his life (vv. 3–6).

III. Shortly thereafter, Sapphira came after Ananias, unaware of what had happened. She was confronted by Peter with the same questions asked of Ananias, and she responded with the same distortions of the truth. Sapphira met her husband's fate (vv. 7–10).

IV. The ultimate disciplinary action had its own singular effect on the church (v. 11).

Case Description

(Recording of Acts 5:1–11)

A Comparable Scriptural Reference

Malachi 3:7–12

Issues and Problems Raised

1. Several issues present themselves, including the matter of stewardship, support of the church, and of course, the inevitable problems arising from misrepresentation of the truth. However, the issue of blasphemy towers over all these. Can you explain what there is about this case that makes it a study in blasphemy?

A Contemporary Situation Suggested by This Case

Statement of Intent

1. We would like to determine from the facts presented what makes the lies of both Ananias and Sapphira blasphemous.

The Principles Governing Our Judgments and Decisions

1. "Be not deceived; God is not mocked: for whatsoever a man soweth, that shall he also reap" (Gal. 6:7). "Let no man deceive you with vain words: for

because of these things cometh the wrath of God upon the children of disobedience" (Eph. 5:6).

Discussion Questions

1. We often rationalize our actions with the self-deceiving question, "Who's going to know the difference, anyway? What is at the bottom of that rationalization?

Decisions and Solutions Suggested

Case Review: An Assessment

Consider Carefully
Acts 15:1–21

Case Study Outline

Introduction: Although great men of the early church gathered at Jerusalem over the issue of the ceremonial law as it applied to circumcision, this meeting could hardly be classified as a church convention. It was a gathering of concerned Christians who, in the company of Peter, Paul, Barnabas, James, and Titus, came to grips with an issue that was to have decisive bearing on the life of the New Testament church.

I. Strife arises in the fledgling New Testament church (ca. 20 years after Pentecost), and a determination is made to discuss the issue, centering initially on circumcision. The meeting is held at Jerusalem (vv. 1–4).

II. The apostles, elders, and various delegations consider the issues as they were interpreted by the Jewish and Gentile members of the church (vv. 5–11).

III. Peter, and especially James, lead the apostles in discussing, and finally agreeing on a course of action in accord with God's New Covenant (vv. 12–21).

Case Description

(Recording of Acts 15:1–21)

A Comparable Scriptural Reference

Amos 9:11–12

A Contemporary Situation Suggested by This Case

Statement of Intent

1. Bible class members will examine controversies they themselves have experienced in the church, list several, and compare how the controversy was handled with the case study presented. They will also list the procedures

followed, the outcomes, and the dynamics of the interpersonal relationships involved.

The Principles Governing Our Judgments and Decisions

1. Controversy over issues in the church call for careful consideration and Gospel-motivated decisions.

Discussion Questions

1. What prior preparations can we make for dealing with controversial issues?

Issues and Problems Raised

1. The criteria we establish to judge events or concerns are critically important. The problem at this council was not about dedication or service to God; that was unquestioned. At issue was the theological premise on which decisions should be made and actions taken.

Decisions and Suggested Solutions

Case Review: An Assessment

16

A Few Contemporary Case Studies

Archie's Dad

Case Description

Archie is the eldest of four brothers and sisters in their teens. He is a college freshman who will undoubtedly make it big in football as a defensive player. At home during the summer months he is, however, involved in a crippling injury at work. Now his football career is not only over, but his college education is also threatened, and the additional burden on the family threatens to destabilize an already weakened financial situation. The family turns to their very close neighbor friends for help and advice. The neighbors, instead of offering any direct advice, tell them they will pray for their spiritual and material welfare, and will also bring their needs to the attention of their church's vestry board. Archie's dad greets this totally unexpected reaction angrily with: "All these years we've known each other, and you know I'm not much for the church thing. Now you want to lay that trip on me. Fine friends you turned out to be!"

Issues and Problems to Be Discussed

Biblical References That Apply to This Case

Goals to Be Pursued in Evaluating This Case

Principles Governing Our Decisions and Judgments

Decisions and Suggested Solutions

Case Study Review: An Assessment

Figure 9   Sample Contemporary Case Study Layout

Archie's Dad

The Case Description

Archie is the eldest of four brothers and sisters in their teens. He is a college freshman who will undoubtedly make it big in football as a defensive player. At home during the summer months he is, however, involved in a crippling injury at work. Now his football career is not only over, but his collge education is also threatened, and the additional burden on the family threatens to destabilize an already weakened financial situation. The family turns to their very close neighbor friends for help and advice. The neighbors, instead of offering any direct advice, tell them they will pray for their spiritual and material welfare, and will also bring their needs to the attention of their church's vestry board. Archie's dad greets this totally unexpected reaction angrily with: "All these years we've known each other, and you know I'm not much for the church thing. Now you want to lay that trip on me. Fine friends you turned out to be!"

Issues and Problems to Be Discussed

Biblical References That Apply to This Case

Goals to Be Pursued in Evaluating This Case

Principles Governing Our Decisions and Judgments

Decisions and Suggested Solutions

Case Study Review: An Assessment

Angie

Case Description

Angie is a second-grader. She is the youngest member of a fine, extended family consisting of Angie's mother and dad, her grandfather, her sister and brother. Her sister Pam, 15, and her brother Babe, 13, have excelled in school and are very much involved in a number of youth activities in the community, school, and church. Angie, however, is another story. She's a gifted girl but barely scratches the surface of her potential. At school she is constantly talking, she is in and out of her seat, and she disrupts her class regularly. During a parent-teacher conference her parents reveal that Angie is their problem-child.

Issues and Problems to Be Discussed:

Biblical References That Apply to This Case:

Goals to Be Pursued in Evaluating This Case:

Principles Governing Our Decisions and Judgments:

Decisions and Suggested Solutions:

Case Study Review: An Assessment

Tony and Jill

Case Description

Tony just cannot seem to relax. He worries about his job, his marriage, the future, and especially about God. At twenty-eight, he seems to be well on his way to a successful career and has impressed many with his hard-driving, self-disciplined work, but his wife Jill feels that if he keeps up the way he is going there will be real danger ahead despite these outward appearances of success and well-being. Jill and Tony have been able to talk over at least some of their anxieties and problems, but every time the subject gets around to church and God, Tony hits the ceiling. Though they attend services together from time to time, Jill is dissatisfied with her faith-life, and Tony seems to be almost petrified of "the tough man upstairs."

Issues and Problems to Be Discussed:

Biblical References That Apply to This Case:

Goals to Be Pursued in Evaluating This Case:

Principles Governing Our Decisions and Judgments:

Decisions and Suggested Solutions:

Case Study Review: An Assessment

Crackup

Case Description

Crossing the mountains in a snowstorm a commuter flight crashes near the timberline. There happen to be two diabetics aboard who have miraculously been thrown out of danger by the crash and have emerged almost unscathed. They do what they can to assist the injured, and, under the direction of a surviving steward, they prepare for the hours ahead as best they can. A short time later one of the diabetics notices that the other is injecting herself with insulin. The shocking realization strikes him at that point: he has not brought his equipment along because of the short commuter flight. He is due, within a matter of hours, for his own shot of insulin. He resolves not to reveal his condition and, undetected, successfully steals the young lady's insulin pouch while she is hunting up firewood. When she returns she finds that her insulin pouch is missing. Along with a few other Christians, she joins a prayer circle, and discusses her situation with them. Though he is an atheist, the other diabetic cannot afford *not* to know what is going on, so he joins the group.

Issues and Problems to Be Discussed:

Biblical References That Apply to This Case:

Goals to Be Pursued in Evaluating This Case:

Principles Governing Our Decisions and Judgments:

Decisions and Suggested Solutions:

Case Study Review: An Assessment:

Appendix A

Lecturing to Lecturers About Lecturing

There is something about lecturing to lecturers that is powerfully suggestive of the ironies involved in carrying coals to Newcastle. Under such circumstances one had better (a) know one's stuff or (b) be something of an intrepid adventurer or (c) be thick-skinned and foolhardy or (d) be all of these—and in huge doses! For if there is one thing about learning and teaching all pastors know and have experienced it is the lecture. But even though we may have some reservations about lectures and lecturing, this particular session on the lecture-discussion Bible study is organized around—you guessed it—a lecture!

When the district adult education committee discussed adult Bible study it was determined that it might be wise to begin any discussion involving pastors and teachers from a realistic point of departure, i.e., that most organized Bible study in our parishes is conducted on the lecture-discussion basis. Analyzing that system and providing a forum for discussing it, thus, necessarily became the first order of business. Time later for the more esoteric. Let's recognize and deal with where we're at; so went the conventional wisdom of your district's think-tank on adult Bible study.

So we find ourselves confronted with the task of considering this age-old system afresh. And it won't do a bit of harm to approach it with the never-say-die spirit of the optimist who said, "Everything's OK so far," as he passed the sixteenth floor of the burning building from which he had just jumped!

Over the years lectures, lecturers, lecture material, and audiences have been exhaustively researched. Consequently, there is no dirth of material. From it a good many guidelines, inferences, and speeches (of course) have been drawn. Two of the more perceptive statements I have seen on the subject follow.

1. The first of these is from an analysis of a gifted historian's style.

A lecture presented to a Pastoral Conference at Logansport, Ind. May 1981.

Note the parallels between historian Frederick J. Turner's style and the fairly characteristic style of parish pastors in adult Bible class settings. Dr. Turner, for your information, was one of America's premier lecturers in history at Wisconsin University and at other places during the latter years of the nineteenth century. The following description of Turner at work is taken from the notes of Dr. Carl Becker, a student of Turner's.

> The lecture itself, if that is the word for it, seemed never prepared, never studiously got-up under the lamp. It seemed rather the spontaneous result of preparation always going on and never finished. The lecture was just an informal, intimately conversational talk, beginning and ending in an interesting manner; always serious without ever being solemn, enlivened with humor and wholesome infectious laughter, yet never falling to the level of the sad professional joke; running off into relevant digressions occasioned by some query; coming back again to the main point; coming now and again to the full stop while notes were eagerly sought out or finished off.
>
> But no—lecture isn't the word . . . An ordered body of information I could get, and often did on my own; but from no other man did I ever get in quite the same measure, that sense of watching a first-class mind at work on its own account, and not merely rehearsing for the benefit of others. It was the delighted sense in the world of sitting there waiting for ideas to be born; waiting for secret meanings; awaiting that convenient explanatory hypothesis to be discovered—lurking as like as not under the dullest mass of drab facts ever seen.

2. But there is, of course, another viewpoint, and it is sharply critical, if not downright testy. Check this statement from a recent work by Professor Walter Kaufmann, *The Future of the Humanities* (1977).

> Lectures are highly problematical and most of them are certainly a waste of time. If the lecturer does not write them out chances are that they will be greatly inferior to something available in print that could be assigned instead. And if he does write them out there seems to be no need for him to read them off because they could easily be made available to the students to read for themselves in half the time.
>
> Does it make sense for people who are bad at lecturing to go right on doing it for decades and alienating students? It seems obvious that at the very least something should be done to decrease the percentage of poor lecturers. But in fact there are thousands of colleges in North America alone, and hardly any of them have given their professor lecturers any advice, not to speak of instruction, about the art with which they earn their living! I doubt that the great majority of them has ever given much thought to the point and aims of lecturing.
>
> What, if anything, can be achieved in this way that could not be done far better by adding another assignment?

These two characteristics come, admittedly, from the formalized setting of academia, the kind of situation we all recall so well from college, university, and seminary days. Our first inclination is to suggest that the parish situation is far different, and that intuition is, of course, right on target. Yet if it is so different, then why is it more often than not treated as though settings such as the Bible class actually *were* academia. The apparent paradox is well worth pondering. Could it be that expectations, presentations, capabilities, and settings are seriously out of synch? Are we yearning for something the situation and the lecturer actually cannot produce?

These two characterizations by Becker and Kaufmann provide us with contrasting viewpoints. Somehow, our task is to steer material, learners, and lecturers away from evils portrayed by Kaufmann and toward the beneficial results Becker recognized in the talented Turner. Again, on the one hand, the lecture has undeniable potential for learning, as well as for artful teaching, and the ensuing learning can certainly be both meaningful and enduring. On the other, the pitfalls seem to warn of impending disaster, a disaster both known and feared: bored learners (if indeed boredom and learning are simultaneously possible); few participants (adults do their voting with their feet we are regularly reminded); or totally passive and dependent learners.

It seems prudent, then, to investigate the strengths and weaknesses, the potential for significant learning, and above all, the pitfalls to avoid. Having done that, we might be in a more advantageous position to address the parish situation.

Let us take the strengths first, hoping to find enough to offset a weakness or three—at very least—and hoping further to offset the chagrin we might feel should it become evident that, having surveyed strengths and weaknesses, the realization might come crushing down on us that we have been doing something less productive than might have been possible with different methodologies—perish the thought!

To begin with, in the teaching-learning situation two fundamental methodologies exist: presentation and exploration. In the lecture we have a strategy that falls within the purview of presentation methodology. Lecturing is labeled a strategy because it is used primarily to serve a style of teaching associated with the presentation of material in one form or another (e.g., film is another form of presentation). The basic underlying assumption in presentation is that the presenter has information or expertise that the listener or observer would (probably) like to have and can get more efficiently and directly from the presenter. Enter the lecture—that classic, enduring, much argued-over strategy.

Its prominent strong points include:

1. A capability for introducing a new topic, field of study, or basic information in an organized, well-worded statement, enabling the hearer to organize future work or study on the basis of the information received.
2. A capability for enabling large audiences to receive pertinent information quickly, in a straightforward way, especially about aspects of concepts or facts, or other material that will be of benefit for that which lies ahead.
3. A strength in conveying information, especially concerning the knowledge and understanding aspects of the cognitive domain of learning.
4. The lecture can, in the hands of articulate and gifted artists, be not only informative, but entertaining and even inspiring, and these are elements which should not be overlooked in any learning situation (Becker's account of Turner's brilliance is a case in point).

These four comprise the list. No more, you ask? Indeed, the list is short. But that need not dismay us *if* there is in it what the philosopher might call elegance, his nomenclature for what is self-sustaining, of quality substance.

And now for the bad news:

1. In the cognitive domain of learning (the others, as you recall, are skills and attitudes), higher levels of intellectual demand are almost impossible to achieve. Thus, analyzing, hypothesizing, problem solving, or evaluating cannot readily be achieved. Regarding the other two domains, it is well-nigh impossible to expect that skills and attitudes can be learned.
2. Because the lecture of necessity must assume that all hearers are at the same relative position with regard to prior knowledge, experience, and basic skills germane to the subject under consideration, the lecture can be expected to be effective only when audiences actually possess those characteristics. If such is *not* the case, the lecture will have spotty, inconsistent results, producing gaps and tending to make the rich richer, and the poor poorer.
3. Two specters sometimes haunt the lecture hall: (a) an arrogance on the part of some lecturers that causes them to disregard, if not disdain, the poor uninformed, and (b) boredom on the part of the listener who, for reasons just or unjust, good or bad, turns off the lecturer despite artful lecturing, or possibly because of inept lecturing.
4. In the lecture setting the very passivity of the hearer may argue against learning of an enduring nature. For reasons we can best identify in theological terms, we humans are whimsical learners. Our attention span at best is precariously short. Of course, one's definition of an active or passive learner is critical at this juncture, but if the aim in learning is to produce an active participant who has a hand in his or her educational destiny, the lecture cannot long serve that purpose effectively or efficiently.

So there we have it: at least some of the major features vying for consideration and outlined in such a way as to suggest an approach to lecture usage that will at least forewarn us as to its potential either to enhance or to detract from learning in the Bible class situation. Permit me to repeat that latter thought, for it contains a sturdy foundation piece for any consideration of purpose, method, or outcome in parish Bible study: learning potential, that is the key item which, at bottom, colors and guides the study of the Word.

It is in our consideration of the potential for learning from the Scripture in the parish Bible class, that the entire range of teaching skills, organization, our expectations, our standards, *and our parishioners as learners* comes clearly into view and engages our careful attention. Consequently, we seek to put this discussion on a different pivot point. We shall not consider ways and means to lecture or to make more clever use of lecture-discussion, but rather: What are the ways in which this style can best be used to serve the learner? Put another way: How can a lecture-discussion style be most strategically used to achieve given purposes in a given situation?

Answers to these questions will vary from pastor to pastor, from parish to parish. No one or single remedy can be dispensed once for all. Learning, as well we know, proceeds in uneven bumps and starts, an adventure if ever there was one! Therefore, answers to ways and means are best discovered and applied individually and in individualistic ways. That suggests quite strongly that a judicious blend of perceived and stated need, along with known or ascribed needs, will turn out to be the right blend for the world's best Bible class—to paraphrase a vintage commercial. So we face first the question: How does one get at these needs? And the answer: Either through informal means (discussion, question/answer, interview, and the like) or formal (through the use of diagnostic instruments from time to time) or a combination of both.

By using diagnostic instruments, along with a careful observation of discussion, local preferences, and rather obvious pastoral needs which present themselves, a parish planning committee is in an excellent position to address its constituency at the point of exposed nerve endings, where maximum interest is stirred, and where the greatest learning potential lies. Did I say parish planning committee? *Does* your adult education committee meet for planning? A second implication, before the class even sets sail, What support systems exist? What organizational arrangements serve the parish Bible class? To what extent can it actually be called a class in which the primary intent is to learn? Those *should* be vexing if not provocative questions.

After the vitally necessary preliminaries, the next considerations, and they are by no means inconsequential, have to do with the standards and purposes teacher and class have in mind as they engage one another in the Bible class setting. Have these been stated in terms both precise and understood by the learners? "Precise," a word purposefully used to forewarn that statements like "to grow in the faith" and "learn about God's Word," however proper and pious sounding, simply will not do, precisely because an articulation of purpose provides direction, and further, to suggest aims that in turn may outline the ways and means to get the job done.

Getting the job done is one thing; how well it is done is another, and introduces the quality component. That necessarily engages teachers and learners in the standards they set. What is the quality control element that guides principle and action in the parish Bible class? Do we actually look for outcomes? What kinds? Have we stated how well or how much with regard to these outcomes?

Not until all these considerations are in place do we dare consider the methods we will use to achieve all of it, even though we may be weighing the merits of a method as we consider these preliminaries. Assuming, however, that the ship is on course and its sails filled with a favorable wind, let's move on to the class session in progress.

This rather brief look will emphasize conditions under which a lecture-discussion type class will probably thrive best. Two major issues commend themselves for consideration in this regard:

1. The three fundamentals on which most all lecture-discussion Bible classes are based are: (a) the well-organized lecture, (b) skillful handling of discussions, and (c) a skillful use of questioning.
2. The lecture-discussion is based upon some rather fundamental

premises: (a) The class usually needs some basic knowledge about the pertinent facts and thrust of information as contained in Scripture or in a doctrine. (b) Goals, information, questions, and summary are indicated with the intention of presenting and clarifying the information, understanding it, and then reviewing it for command of the material. *Note:* purpose, meaning, and comprehension are the only real learning aims in mind. We may suppose that skills could become a part of future learning, based on the information presented.

Thus, within the admittedly limited range, the lecture-discussion can be appropriately used as an effective strategy. It is a wholly different story, however, when it comes to skill teaching and in the area of attitude, value, and priority selection. These domains cannot readily or effectively be taught through the medium of lecture. Evangelism is a case in point. It is, at bottom, a skill. As such, we have learned during the seventies, in a fervor of hectic activity, that doing was a big part of learning, and that meant getting-out-there-on-the-doorstep. The inference for teaching is loud and clear. One simply does not teach skills via the lecture. Likewise, there are other ways and means much better suited for teaching value system and priority selection.

All things considered, then, the lecture-discussion strategy, a time-honored part of presentation methodology, is, alas, a strategy of limited potential. Once having overcome the shock of hearing that, you may well want to consider sending me to the nearest lock-up. But before you do, kindly reconsider that while its strong points are sine qua non to cognitive learning, it is still limited in that it can only serve the purpose of exposing people to factual information, and beyond that, of being of some limited assistance in comprehending or understanding the information.

And of equally crucial importance, is the consideration of the learner and the learning context within which all these aims are to be fulfilled in the Bible class setting. We return, in conclusion to some bothersome, recurring questions.

1. Is what we are doing as teaching pastors consistent with the purpose, learners, and context of the situation?
2. Do we know, beyond an educated guess what the actual, perceived, and educational needs and goals of the learners are?
3. Do we possess some way or means of discovering, beyond calculated estimation, what the learner takes away from the Bible class session into everyday living?
4. Is the different-strokes-for-different-folks phenomenon a part of your parish educational structure?
5. Do our efforts actually contribute to the making of a Scripture-wise, knowledgeable, skillful, and priority-conscious Body of Christ—in the educational setting?

God grant His continuing blessing upon your many labors as you serve Him faithfully in your vital ministry among His people!

Appendix **B**

Concerning Questions and Question-Asking Skills

Question Categories

Category A	Category B
Narrow-Range Questions	*Broad-Range Questions*
Cognitive Memory Types Convergent Types	Divergent Types Evaluate Types

The narrow range of questions requires short, factual answers, or other, fairly predictable answers. They allow for only a limited range of correct answers. Cognitive memory questions simply request the respondent to repeat remembered information. It is the most often used question in classroom settings, accounting for approximately 70 percent of all question-asking activity. Convergent questions require the respondent to put facts together and to construct an answer. It is a narrow-range question because it requires a single best, or accurate answer. Approximately 85 percent of all questioning activity is done in the narrow range.

The broad range of questions permits a variety of acceptable responses. They cause the respondent to predict, infer, judge, or hypothesize. These types usually initiate high-level thinking processes. Divergent questions require that the respondent organize elements or data into new patterns that may not have been previously recognized.

Evaluative questions request answers based on judgments, the defense of a position or value, or the justification of a choice. Broad-range questions require prior and sometimes substantial preparation.

Suggestions for Skillful Questioning

1. Know each question type and its potential.
2. Phrase questions so that they will elicit information, not threaten the personhood of the responder.
3. Phrase questions so that they will not be ambiguous.
4. Phrase questions to that they will not confuse the responder.
5. Refine the responses to your questions so that further thinking will be encouraged.
6. Phrase questions without undue bias or inference that might color the response before it is given.
7. High-level thinking is encouraged by questions that begin with: What are the ways in which . . . ? How can . . . ?

Appendix C

Instructional Responsibility:
A Developmental Look

The instructional task involves teachers and learners in a number of interrelated and developmental progressions. These progressions, with their accompanying instructional responsibilities, are outlined below. Each of the domains of learning is represented, as well as the status and participation level of the learner.

Category	From	To	Instructional Responsibility
Cognitive Domain of Learning (Knowledge)	An uninformed status	An appropriately and reasonably acceptable informed status	Clear, straightforward, well-organized arrangement of essential information; monitor grasp of accuracy and control of information.
Conative Domain of Learning (Skill)	An unskilled performer	An appropriate level of performing ability	Analyze and demonstrate in a variety of ways the mental or physical skill; provide opportunity for the learner to perform the skill under instructional control until the skill is mastered.
Affective Domain of Learning (Attitude)	Inconsistent and tentatively developed value system	Actions consistent with established and preferred priorities in value and life-styles	Provide instructional opportunities to analyze systems, personal priorities, and circumstances involving choice.
Participation and Status	Limited participation in the process and quite dependent as a learner	Active participant and contributor in the process and relatively independent as a learner	Of the two categories of instructional methodolgy (presentational and explorational), the presentational methods tend to dominate at initial stages, giving way gradually to explorational.

Appendix D

The Affective Domain

Each of the domains of learning may be differentiated according to:

Typical *Ways of Feeling or Expressing Emotion*	*Affective or Attitude Domain*
Typical Ways of Thinking	Cognitive Domain
Typical Ways of Acting or Doing	Conative or Skill Domain

A hierarchial arrangement similar to that of the cognitive domain has been developed for the affective domain, as follows:

1. *Receiving* At the lower level of the domain's hierarchy is receiving. Awareness, a willingness to receive, and controlled attention are component parts of this initial stage. In order for a value or priority to be established, one must first be in a position to receive, pay attention, and consciously absorb the essence of the value being presented. Should one not even be predisposed to receive the value or priority, it will be next to impossible to have it incorporated into the thought pattern and lifestyle of the learner.
2. *Responding* A positive and further step beyond reception is that of responding, a clearcut indication that the value or priority is, in the mind of the learner, worth sustained consideration, if not adaptation. A willingness to respond and a satisfaction in the response are important parts of this level.
3. *Valuing* At the heart of this domain is an accepted value or preferred choosing (priority selection). When the learner has not only received, but responded to the value presented, it is highly

probable that he will not only accept and prefer that value, but commit himself to it. The usual order is: accepting the value; preferring the value; and committing to the value.

4. *Organizing* When the value or priority has been accepted, preferred, and finally has become a commitment, a new order of doing things is arranged in the person's life accordingly. Conceptualizing the value and organizing one's life according to the value system are the major issues involved at this level.

5. *Being Characterized by, or Identified Completely with, the Value.* In this final stage, the value has been fully incorporated into the learner's life so that it is possible to characterize his style and being according to the dictates of the value or priority.

Affective Characteristics Summarized:

1. These have to do with feelings.
2. In each person these feelings are usually manifested in typical ways.
3. These feelings possess a degree of intensity.
4. These feelings imply direction (direction in this setting meaning: along a continuum from negative to positive).
5. There is always a target or object for the feeling.

Affective Characteristics Tend to Be Related to:

1. attentiveness and interest
2. willingness to persist
3. cooperation—disruption
4. achievement—lack of achievement
5. a locus of control, meaning: The individual assumes responsibility for behavior (locus is internal); responsibility for behavior is beyond or outside the individual (locus is external).

Cognitive Dissonance

A person receives a message, information, value proposal, that is dissonant (i.e., contradicts) with established beliefs. This dissonance sets up a tension within the individual that is finally relieved in one of several ways. The three more typical reactions include:

1. rejection, sometimes immediately, sometimes after enough of the possibility is presented so as to give the learner a reliable concept of the proposed value;
2. an attempt to adapt, endeavoring to include the best of both worlds, most often unsuccessful;
3. a reordering of value structure and priorities according to the new value presented; a surrender, as it were, to a new order or set of values/priorities.

Closely Related Areas of Consideration

1. *Motivation,* which has as its major components, attention, interest, and concentration.
2. *Predisposition, Bias, Unalterable Commitment,* all of which become involved as parts of the total picture directly affecting the possibility of acquiring new or different patterns or of ultimately rejecting them.

Credits:

David Kratwohl, Benjamin Bloom, and Bertram Masia: *Taxonomy of Education Objectives, Handbook II: Affective Domain*
Leon Festinger, *Cognitive Dissonance*

Helpful Resources and References

Books

Adams, J.; Hayes, J.; and Hopson, B. *Transition: Understanding and Managing Personal Change*. London: M. Robertson, 1976.

Agnew, M. *Future Shapes of Adult Religious Education*. New York: The Paulist Press, 1976.

Apps, Jerold. *Problems in Continuing Education*. New York: McGraw-Hill Book Co., 1979.

Aslanian, Carol B., and Brickell, H. M. *Americans in Transition: Life Changes as Reasons for Adult Learning*. New York: College Entrance Examination Board, 1980.

Bergevin, Paul, and McKinley, John. *Design for Adult Education in the Church*. New York: The Seabury Press, 1958.

Brophy, Jere E., and Evertson, Carolyn M. *Learning from Teaching: A Developmental Perspective*. Boston: Allyn and Bacon, 1976.

Coleman, Lucien. *How to Teach the Bible*. Nashville: Broadman Press, 1979.

Cross, K. Patricia. *Adults as Learners*. San Francisco: Jossey-Bass Publishers, 1981.

Elias, John L. *The Foundations and Practice of Adult Religious Education*. Malabar, Fla.: Robert Krieger Publishing Company, 1982.

Erikson, Erik, ed. *Adulthood*. New York: W. W. Norton, 1978.

Feucht, Oscar E. *Learning to Use Your Bible*. St. Louis: Concordia Publishing House, 1969.

Ford, LeRoy. *Design for Teaching and Training*. Nashville: Broadman Press, 1978.

Fowler, James. *Stages of Faith*. New York: Harper & Row, 1981.

Hyman, Ronald. *Strategic Questioning*. Englewood Cliffs, N. J.: Prentice-Hall, 1979.

Knox, Alan B. and Associates. *Developing, Administering, and Evaluating Adult Education*. San Francisco: Jossey-Bass Publishers, 1980.

Lawson, Kenneth, H. *Philosophical Concepts and Values in Adult Education*. Nottingham, Eng.: Barnes and Humby, 1975.

Lockyer, Herbert. *All About Bible Study*. Grand Rapids: Zondervan, 1977.

Long, Huey; Hiemstra, Roger; and Associates. *Changing Approaches to Studying Adult Education*. San Francisco: Jossey-Bass Publishers, 1980.

Mansoor, Menahem. *The Dead Sea Scrolls* (2nd ed.). Grand Rapids: Baker Book House, 1983.

McKenzie, Leon. *Adult Religious Education*. West Mystic, Conn.; Twenty-Third Publications, 1977.

Metcalf, William. *16 Methods of Group Bible Study*. Valley Forge, Pa.; Judson Press, 1980.

Moran, Gabriel. *Education Toward Adulthood: Religion and Lifelong Learning*. New York: The Paulist Press, 1979.

Richards, Lawrence O. *Creative Bible Teaching*. Chicago: Moody Press, 1980.

Sheehy, Gail. *Passages: Predictable Passages in Life*, New York: E. P. Dutton, 1976.

Stonehouse, Catherine M. *Patterns in Moral Development*. Waco. Word, 1980.

Suelflow, Roy. *Christian Churches in Recent Times*. St. Louis: Concordia Publishing House, 1980.

Taylor, Marvin, ed. *Foundations for Christian Education in an Era of Change*. Nashville: Broadman Press, 1978.

Thompson, Norma H., ed. *Religious Education and Theology*. Birmingham: Religious Education Press, 1982.

Tough, Allen. *Intentional Changes*. Chicago: Follett Publishing Co., 1982.

Ward, Ted. *Values Begin at Home*. Wheaton: Scripture Press, 1979

Wilbert, Warren N. *Teaching Christian Adults*, Grand Rapids: Baker Book House, 1980.

Bible Study Helps

Aharoni, Y.; and Avi-Yonah, M. *MacMillan Bible Atlas*. New York: The MacMillan Company, 1977.

Bible Atlas, The. Nashville: Broadman Press, 1975.

Bright, John. *A History of Israel*. Philadelphia: The Westminster Press, 1972.

Concordia Bible Dictionary. St. Louis: Concordia Publishing House, 1963.

Creative Leadership for Teacher Growth, Elgin: David C. Cook Publishing House.

Cruden, Alexander. *Cruden's Unabridged Concordance*. Nashville: Broadman Press, 1965.

Franzmann, Martin A. *The Word of the Lord Grows*. St. Louis: Concordia Publishing House, 1961.

Halley, Henry H. *Halley's Pocket Bible Handbook*, rev. ed. Grand Rapids: Zondervan Publishing House, 1976.

Harper's Bible Dictionary rev. ed. Ed. by Madeleine S. Miller and J. Lane. New York: Harper & Row, 1973.

Nave, Orville. *Nave's Topical Bible*. Grand Rapids: Baker Book House, 1978.

Osborne, Grant R.; and Woodward, Stephen. *Handbook for Bible Study*, Grand Rapids: Baker Book House, 1983.

Oxford Bible Atlas, 2nd ed. New York: Oxford University Press, 1974.

Roehrs, Walter; and Franzmann, Martin A. *The Concordia Self-Study Commentary*. St. Louis: Concordia Publishing House, 1979.

Tenny, Merrill; and Cruden, Alexander. *The Handy Bible Dictionary and Concordance*, Grand Rapids: Zondervan,

Wycliffe Bible Encyclopedia, 2 vols. Ed. by Charles E. Pfeiffer. Chicago: Moody Press, 1975.

525585